Anxiety

Curing the New Normal

Gina Herd, LCSWR

Green Heart Living Press

Anxiety: Curing the New Normal

Copyright © 2023 Gina Herd

All rights reserved. No part of this book may be used or reproduced by any means, graphic, electronic, or mechanical, including photocopying, recording, taping, or by any information storage retrieval system without the written permission of the publisher, except in the case of brief quotations embodied in critical articles and reviews.

ISBN Paperback: 978-1-954493-56-8

Excerpt from "Controlling People" by Patricia Evans, Copyright © 2002 by Patricia Evans. Used with permission of the Publisher. All rights reserved.

Cover design: Barb Pritchard of Infinity Design

Published by Green Heart Living Press.

This book is designed to provide information and motivation to our readers. It is sold with the understanding that the publisher is not engaged to render any type of psychological, legal, or any other kind of professional advice. The content of each article is the sole expression and opinion of its author, and not necessarily that of the publisher. No warranties or guarantees are expressed or implied by the publisher's choice to include any of the content in this volume. Neither the publisher nor the individual author(s) shall be liable for any physical, psychological, emotional, financial, or commercial damages, including, but not limited to, special, incidental, consequential or other damages. Our views and rights are the same: You are responsible for your own choices, actions, and results.

Dedication

This book is dedicated to all my incredible patients
who had the instinct to finish our work together.
You taught me more than you will ever know.
And to the two people I love the most,
Richard and Alexander.

Table of Contents

Introduction	7
Chapter 1: Anxiety is the New Norm	9
Chapter 2: The Depression Train	13
Chapter 3: Living with Anxiety	17
Chapter 4: What Does Anxiety Look Like	21
Chapter 5: The Cure	41
Chapter 6: The Treatment	51
About the Author	159

Introduction

I am sharing my life's work with you. For over 20 years I have read, debated, observed, and tested how and why we get and have anxiety. I came to understand that psychology (really all of life) is about patterns. In order to change the pattern, you must see it and then have an action plan, otherwise, nothing will change. We just don't grow out of our patterns. It's been more than fascinating and shockingly uncomplicated. In working with families, this is where I see the impact, whether that is with two or five members. I believe in family even if that means you must create your own family to find healing. I also believe in love. We can choose to love those who are healthy for us and are not repeating our lifelong abusive patterns.

I have had the drive to make a difference in the lives of families, especially marginalized families, so asking why over the years has been my method. I have read dozens of books on anxiety and control but when I found Patricia Evans' book *Controlling People*, I thought this is the book that describes what I can't say in front of someone who is struggling to think clearly. Ms. Evans does a great job of discussing something that is clinical without knowing she is defining a psychological perspective that affects millions.

What I have written for you is a guide and workbook. Please prepare yourself not to rush through my process. I know very well that when you have anxiety rushing seems the right thing to do, but it is not. Rushing, reading ahead, and speeding through the stages, will not give you the outcome of having reduced or eliminated anxiety. Learning to slow down, think, and feel things is a good thing and it will be okay.

Can you read this book over a 10-month time period? I challenge you to do just that. There is homework along the way. Please trust me on this. To increase your success, I have included a free online group. In this group, I will reinforce the basics of the treatment, coach you and answer your questions.

Please go to the website www.ginaherdlcsw.com and register. You will also find additional support there as you move through the stages of the work. I am here in support of you and am on your success team.

Chapter 1
Anxiety is the New Norm

I have had more questions than answers in my 17-year psychotherapy practice and in my personal life. Why do 70% of people in the United States have a mental illness? Why do we hit and/or verbally degrade our children and are not even aware we are doing this? When our children have issues, why do we look to others and not ourselves? Why is controlling one another now the new norm for interpersonal relationships even when it's blatantly problematic? And, most hauntingly, why are our children committing random acts of severe violence (murder or suicide) and we insist it is due to cell phones, schools, or guns?

The answer is that they suffer from anxiety and depression. That anxiety is taught by their parental figures.

By definition, depression is unclear thinking. It has many other descriptions but at its basic, it is the inability to see and think clearly on an ongoing basis. Let's agree that anxiety is negative thinking. Also, it is ongoing, each and every day, all day. How does that translate into our everyday lives? What does it look like when we parent, when we have conversations, when we make big and small decisions, and even just making plans to be social or in business? When we experience anxiety and depression, we function on a very primitive level. We normalize our bad behavior and assign blame to minor obstacles as to why we are unable to complete goals.

It is clear to me that my profession is joining in the movement to excuse bad and inappropriate behavior, in ourselves and in our society. According to CNN Health in partnership with Kaiser Family Health Foundation a poll of American adults report that 90% of those adults believe that there is a mental health crisis in the United States today. It must make sense this includes the people in the mental health profession. When we, as mental health professionals, parents, friends, and community members, excuse seemingly minor offenses, we pave the way for more heinous acts. We are in effect condoning more and more violence and primitive behaviors. The problem with accepting these low-priority behaviors is that they increase the bar for much more serious offenses such as physical abuse and murder.

We see this clearly in the constant violent acts by children (mostly under 24 years old). We continue to grieve and then quickly move on without looking at the root cause.

In 2014 Prime Minister David Cameron stated, "We will never defeat Isis until we get to the root cause." We also will not decrease child violence until we address the root cause. We are settling for management of our anxiety and depression and not a cure and long-term stability.

When I began writing this in 2013 that was the thought process that was being generated here in the United States. Today we are coming out of a pandemic and because we began with a high amount of anxiety and depression we are now triggered to greater and more overt mental illness. When thousands die (mostly young people) because we believe we can do nothing and then we find a solution and we are still dying; this is what depression and anxiety look like day to day.

The Diagnostic and Statistical Manual (DSM-IV) definition of generalized anxiety disorder (GAD) is excessive anxiety and worry (apprehensive expectation), occurring more days than not for at least six months. This definition does not even come close to identifying let alone understanding anxiety.

I am shocked that no one is acknowledging what anxiety really looks like.

The good news is when we define anxiety correctly, we are easily able to treat and improve this debilitating mental illness.

The challenge is to address the root cause of anxiety and not the superficial. I do see that most people with anxiety think the entire world has anxiety and that would stand to reason since anxiety is a system of negative thinking that takes over your life. Who could bear to be around that unless you also had anxiety?

Chapter 2

The Depression Train

If you look at my depression train you can understand why in America crime and violence have increased since the pandemic.

Stops on the Depression Train

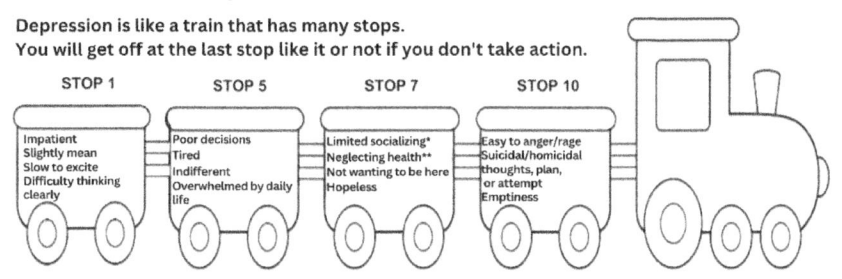

Depression is like a train that has many stops.
You will get off at the last stop like it or not if you don't take action.

STOP 1
- Impatient
- Slightly mean
- Slow to excite
- Difficulty thinking clearly

STOP 5
- Poor decisions
- Tired
- Indifferent
- Overwhelmed by daily life

STOP 7
- Limited socializing*
- Neglecting health**
- Not wanting to be here
- Hopeless

STOP 10
- Easy to anger/rage
- Suicidal/homicidal thoughts, plan, or attempt
- Emptiness

Key words:
*Limited socializing: Regular outings with friends or partner, NOT including family.
** Neglected health: Not cleaning body. Not going to dentist or medical providers regularly.

Let's say that as a society prior to the pandemic, we were at a 5. (Americans have had an exceedingly high rate of depression and anxiety). At that level, when something comes along triggering such as a life-changing, life-altering pandemic we are now triggered to a much higher number, say 6, 7, or even 8. Because of that number, you will see violence, people not thinking clearly, strange and bizarre things happening. Yet somehow, we cannot, are not and do not want to look at why that is occurring. If we had relatively low rates of anxiety and depression prior to the pandemic, let's say a 2, the pandemic would certainly be triggering but we would be at a much lower number (perhaps a 3 or 4) and therefore the behaviors and the manifestation of our anxiety and depression would not be as dangerous and life-threatening.

Suicide and drug-related death rates have risen to extreme and unprecedented numbers, and it is still a conversation we are not able to have. We are not understanding how mental illness works and where it comes from and how to treat it as a society. We are not alone in being triggered and we look at things that are going on in the world, random acts of the need to control at all costs such as the situation in Ukraine.

The higher the number on the Depression Train the higher the level of mental illness the more difficult it is to reset it to a lower number and to then reinvent ourselves. To reset is to find Joy. This Joy will never come from anything outside of ourselves. It will never come from things. It *will* come from being fulfilled by nature and by the people that we say we love.

One of the first things my cured patients tell me is that the friends they once had are difficult and hard to be around. Frequently they are argumentative, complaining, and just not happy. They are convinced that this is just how the world functions or "their" world in any case. This method of thinking is learned in childhood and so the child grows up with what they have learned in a backwards way as truth.

I started my journey by looking at why people are controlling as a social scientist, from a scientific point of view. I had so many questions. Why do people abuse their children, their partners, the very people they say they love? Why is it so difficult for us to remain in intimate relationships? Why don't we have

The Depression Train

an accurate definition of what abuse looks like today in the 21st century? At present, 25 years after my education, it appears as if I am living in a world in which 75% of the people (maybe more) are walking backwards. I liken walking backwards to people falling because they cannot see clearly, running into one another, hurting one another, hurting themselves, and there is blood running down their necks, their faces, and their extremities. They are in such pain, and we normalize it.

Yet, to merely say to them, "Why are you in such pain? Do you not see the root of your pain? You are walking backwards!" Saying things like this only causes more pain. We are in a world in which we refuse to look at how we can simplify things such as allowing nature to help you parent your child and to acknowledge your fear-based parenting based on how you were parented.

This can change our entire planet so quickly. But this is not where we are. Instead, we normalize anxiety and depression, we normalize mental illness, and we minimize the role of a mother and father and the influence that they have on the human mind developing before the age of five.

There was a time when it was a difficult thing to get a parent to bring a child into my office before the child started asking for help or an outside source such as a school highly recommended therapy. Today I see three and four-year olds biting their own limbs; their fingers, their hands until they bleed. I see children who cannot focus, sit still for 30 seconds, cannot sleep, cannot eat, all before the age of five years old.

Anxiety: Curing the New Normal

Anxiety is increasing and yet I sit in front of a parent and ask her how much of this she thinks she is responsible for and frequently she says "none."

I can no longer sit by and witness this as a social scientist. We have to do something quickly and begin to condemn our backwards and dangerous thinking.

Having an anxiety disorder is the new norm. When we excuse seemingly minor offenses, we pave the way for more heinous acts. We are in effect condoning more and more violence. The problem with accepting these seemingly low-priority behaviors is that they increase the bar for much more serious offenses such as physical abuse and murder. We see this clearly in the constant violent acts by children (under 24 years old). We continue to grieve and then quickly move on without looking at the origin of this progressive mental illness. We will not decrease child anxiety and depression until we look at the root cause. The "extremist" mindset is one of anxiety. This mindset of control has become our fundamental parenting style, creating a society of anxiety and depression.

I am shocked that no one has accurately identified what anxiety really looks like. When we define it correctly, we are easily able to treat and improve this serious mental illness. Without a proper definition, we are unable to understand anxiety and only management is possible.

ANXIETY=CONTROL=FEAR=NEGATIVE THINKING

Chapter 3
Living with Anxiety

First things first, what is anxiety, and do you have it?

In 2014 Verizon produced a powerful commercial to promote its Girls in Science campaign. The commercial (which can be viewed on YouTube[1]) depicts how fear-based parenting produces anxiety and depression in a child from birth. Fear-based parenting is becoming commonplace and we have the delusion that we are not allowed to criticize one another's parenting styles (not even as professionals) unless the blood is shed of a child (and sometimes not even then). Mental illness is passed down from one generation to the next. With each generation, we see the deeper societal effects resulting in extreme violence and yet we can't accept or see our role in the deterioration of our behavior, let alone our own children's behavior.

The mind and body experience this type of fear-based parenting (it's okay for me as the parent to be afraid of most things; it will not affect my child) as trauma. There is also trauma that causes anxiety that is not related to unaware parenting. Bad things can and do occur in a child's life that cannot be prevented. I am discussing here the trauma that can be prevented which is the majority of what I see in my practice and in society.

---

[1] https://www.youtube.com/watch?v=yND9hDpPwYA

Anxiety is a physical sensation in the body that is consistent and accompanied by the inability to sustain a positive thought, hence the anxiety sufferer is having ongoing conscious or unconscious negative thoughts. This is a constant low level of "fear," which is physical and is always present within them (at different degrees) 24 hours a day. Stress is unlike anxiety in that it is situational: you have a job interview and have been stressed over the preparation the night before but once in the actual interview you are confident and in the moment.

With stress, unlike anxiety, you are not paralyzed with fear. When you suffer from anxiety you think negatively about the interview days prior, during the interview, and days after the interview. This constant fear increases to a point that the body can no longer manage, and the anxiety sufferer begins to have exaggerated symptoms that may mimic a minor medical ailment. (I once had a patient with anxiety that made him blind in one eye.) Anxiety never goes away and those with anxiety sometimes convince themselves that everyone has anxiety and even that their anxiety is part of their personality. Because this condition is learned during childhood, the person is convinced that nothing is wrong or that others are the root of their issues in life.

There are many types of anxiety, but most people suffer from generalized anxiety disorder (GAD). This is a general fear of everything. Even when a person has one specific fear, upon careful exploration you find they have a host of fears that they deem as "normal" and the anxiety sufferer is not even aware that their entire point of view and all of their thoughts and

Living with Anxiety

most of their actions are negative and rooted in negative thinking that they learned in childhood.

In a nutshell, people with anxiety have a fear of losing control. The general fear is a need to control everything and even control the control. Although I am referring to the type of control that dictates the need for things to go a certain way, control takes on a deeper meaning in the context of anxiety.

The role of control in early childhood development has been proven in many sources. A study conducted by Chorpita and Barlow (1998) discusses theories that anxiety plays a central role in learned negative emotions.[2] I reiterate that anxiety is a learned behavior, a process of both thinking and feeling, and anything that can be learned can be unlearned or re-learned.

My profession is now in the business of managing something that is completely curable. Because we are not able to effectively treat it, we are excusing more and more minor yet dangerous pathological behaviors in everyday life. The management of anxiety results in getting rid of or suppressing the physical symptoms only. This leads to making anxiety worse because the suppression of a volcano eventually results in a major eruption. Another challenge is that other pathologies mimic anxiety (for example, schizophrenia and paranoia). We will look more deeply into this in the next chapter.

---

[2] Bruce Chorpita and Davide Barlowe, *The Development of Anxiety: The Role of Control in Early Environment.* APA, 1998.

Chapter 4

What Does Anxiety Look Like?

We have assigned the word "bullying" to a much more serious pathology (similarly done with the word "molest" in child rape). We have this idea that there is a victim and a perpetrator but in the case of bullying or domestic violence this is not true. It is the need for control and negative thinking that we see in "bullying," domestic violence, physical abuse against our children, and in many acts of random violence. If we do not have an accurate description of anxiety, we are not able to understand domestic violence or "bullying" and therefore it continues. It is the need for control, negative thinking, and learned abuse that is the dance of control. The victim has learned not to stand up for themselves from his parents and the perpetrator has learned to control others, that control is love, from his parents. Both now have anxiety. Both now want control: the victim says, "I want control over how you think of me, please like me" and the perpetrator says, "I need to dance (abuse) with someone to feel something in a relationship."

I worked at a domestic violence shelter for many years. This was where I first developed my method for treating anxiety. Part of my job was to hold a weekly group of 15 women. I also met with each of the women individually. Each of them had a shocking story. The first shock was that 12 out of the 15 revealed to me in confidence that they had beaten the male partner and fled to the women's domestic violence shelter in fear of retaliation. The violence to the male partner ranged from stabbing him in his sleep to pouring boiling water on him while he was in the shower.

The other shocking fact I learned was that they beat and abused one another for years and not just with one partner. Each of them had partners in their past in which abuse (verbal, physical, emotional) was part of the relationship.

The most disturbing but telling thing I learned from the women was that they found the chaos comforting and were able to admit that they expected abuse and degradation in their intimate relationships. As I met with them it became clear that their childhoods mimicked their current relationships in all aspects of their lives. They had chaotic and abusive relationships with their children, friends, and intimate partners. Sessions revealed that how they had been treated by their parents/parental figures in childhood was the exact same way their relationships were in adulthood.

As with most mental illnesses they were not able to see the patterns and had limited insight as to what "abuse" looks like. For example: if I beat you (yell at you or leave you to raise yourself) and tell you that I love you then the beating or neglect (all are abusive) becomes love (normal).

I was very young when I worked at the shelter, but this was the beginning of my understanding and seeing the power of parenting over a violent existence as well as fostering anxiety and depression.

What Does Anxiety Look Like?

The women who taught me about anxiety and child development in that shelter system had come from all walks of life. They were educated, uneducated, and of every social economic class and race. The women and children changed names and faces over my years working at the shelter, but they all had the same pathology.

What Anxiety Looks and Feels Like from the Outside In

People who suffer from anxiety have at any given time a specific fear or a multitude of fears that only make sense to them. Below is a list of behaviors and thought patterns that no one talks about when describing or treating anxiety.

<u>Ongoing racing thoughts</u> - These are the constant negative and judgmental thoughts learned in childhood. The thoughts are about how others are judging them, how to please others so that they see the anxiety sufferer in a particular way and a general chaotic process in which the anxiety sufferer thinks through all the possible thoughts of others to get each and every situation perfect. Of course, this is impossible, but they try and this is a cycle that goes nowhere and leaves the anxiety sufferer overwhelmed and unhappy with self and others. This thought process is also degrading in interpersonal relationships.

The racing thought is often the exact same thought going through the mind hundreds of times per day. The person takes that thought on as absolute truth when in fact it usually is not, but the anxiety sufferer is completely convinced that they see clearly. The need to please is actually a need to control.

The anxiety sufferer has the learned belief that if they behave a certain way then they can control the outcome and thoughts and feelings of a multiple of variables in life. The idea of "racing thoughts" is usually misunderstood because it's not a variety of thoughts but at any given time one thought that gets "stuck" in the mind and the sufferer cannot let it go. The thought is also a negative thought which eventually results in violence or degradation to self or others.

Racing thoughts/negative thoughts grow so once they start, they progress in the moment and over time. Usually, the sufferer will have this thought for days or weeks. This makes it almost impossible to do schoolwork or fully hear most conversations. The sufferer also normalizes the negative thoughts as a way to deal with them and also because they were taught this from their parental figures since early childhood.

Negative thoughts are about random people or ideas so much so that anxiety sufferers don't usually know they are negative. Instead, they just feel tired or "not good." They live without inner peace and inner quiet every day all day. A negative thought grows (as does a positive thought) so you will see those with anxiety being verbally overzealous. They often talk in monologues that eventually are negative. They are not only unaware that they are monopolizing a conversation but that they are speaking negatively in their monologue and that it is growing in intensity.

Example: Sean has a new girlfriend who acts kindly, attentively, and is physically and emotionally available to him. Sean and the new girlfriend verbalize their feelings and when an issue arises, it is usually a misunderstanding that is discussed and resolved. Both Sean and his girlfriend let things go easily. Life is not perfect, but they like each other and so they each think positively about one another and give each other "the benefit of the doubt."

If Sean had anxiety, he would be accustomed to a relationship that is judgmental or accusatory so he would begin to create ideas and negative thoughts about the new girlfriend to the extent that he accuses her of disrespecting him and eventually talks himself out of the relationship. Sean would continue to think negatively about the relationship (making it easier for him to refuse all contact with her) and about his life in general, totally convinced he saw the situation clearly and that his point of view was accurate. In fact, it would be the exact opposite, not clear and not accurate. If the girlfriend also had anxiety (which is highly probable because anxiety sufferers are attracted to what is familiar) then she would convince him to love her, and this would be the basis of the relationship complete with constant arguments and chaos.

If the girlfriend had anxiety, then the dynamic would be comfortable for both. The relationship would revolve around constant primitive conversations about control. Both Sean and his girlfriend would fight violently on a regular (usually daily) basis and then makeup. If the couple is very young (under 24 years), they would most likely break up because pathology is progressive, and the arguments would even exceed the learned behavior from childhood.

More importantly, their instincts would tell them that "this" is not "right" and nature would lead them to the idea that "the feelings in this relationship are not natural."

I have to say here that a person with anxiety will find it almost impossible to be with someone who does not have anxiety; they can only feel loved if there is that struggle for control. "I can't love you if you love me" pattern of unconscious thought. And vice versa, the person without anxiety will not understand how a person can think in such a negative backwards way. Reality-based communication is almost impossible with someone who has anxiety.

It is likely that a person with depression can tolerate an anxiety sufferer because they are indifferent and somewhat familiar with negative thinking (more on depression later) so depending on the age of the persons involved the "dance" could cultivate into a relationship. Those dynamics lessen as one gets older as again pathology is progressive.

<u>Exhausted</u> - You will find anxiety sufferers exhausted. This is partly because the need to overthink each detail of life is mentally exhausting but also, they have poor to no boundaries and are unaware of their limitations and needs. A person with anxiety feels the need to say yes to the desires of others to the extent that it interferes with their own life stability. The anxiety sufferer does this because they learned in childhood that this is how to control how others feel about you and to make them like or even love you.

What Does Anxiety Look Like?

They are also exhausted due to lack of sleep. Who can sleep when thinking about all the ways to get control and you live in fear? The fear-based thinking worsens at night because there are no distractions.

Example: Without anxiety an individual works really diligently at their job, stays late as needed, works overtime within their boundaries and is generally committed to their career and situation.

When a person has anxiety, they think negatively about the outcome even though they frequently work at home, stay very late, and allow the employer to infringe on their personal time. They are in pain going over all the ways to prevent themselves from getting fired or reprimanded to the extent that often they are not really doing a good job at all. Each day is long, painful, and negative. They have convinced themselves this is part of their "specific" job and just part of their life.

The person without anxiety says I have boundaries, so I don't work more than my life allows me to. I have my own internal set of goals and standards that push me to be the best. If those around me see my worth, then great and if they don't then it is time for me to move on in any case.

Again, this is about how the anxiety sufferer can control how others (boss and co-workers) think and feel about them.

<u>Immature Thinking/Behavior</u> - People with anxiety have a very difficult time focusing on the idea or situation in front of them so they struggle with daily activities, reading, having full conversations, and progressing in life. Getting stuck on a thought is like the needle on a vinyl LP getting stuck on a record player.

The needle will play the same few words or notes thousands of times, never finishing playing. The emotional and intellectual progress is stunted in the anxiety sufferer, and they are usually not even aware of this process.

If a person is to have racing thoughts for days, weeks, and months, then new ideas that should be getting into the mind are not consistently accepted. It would stand to reason that if an anxiety sufferer has this process over time, even a lifetime, it creates the inability for the mind to mature and explore new ideas. Because they get stuck on thoughts due to the ruminating and ongoing fear, the anxiety sufferer is not hearing entire parts of conversations, lessons, and feedback.

In therapy, this is especially challenging because we must look at the role our parental figures had on our lives. Most adults without anxiety have come to see their parental figures as flawed and that generally occurs naturally during adolescence. Some with anxiety still hold onto being a child (stuck on a thought) and needing the approval of the parental figures no matter if the parent is deceased or the anxiety sufferer is 40 years of age. This need further exacerbates the immaturity.

Immature behavior is also evident in interpersonal relationships. People with anxiety are frequently not able to confront friends or loved ones about their needs and wants. They may run from situations and justify the behavior. Anxiety sufferers are frequently angry at and negative towards others and life situations because others do not behave in a manner that they see fit. They show a lack of patience and therefore are upset when things don't move or happen on their timeline.

You will find that people with anxiety are "childlike," sometimes at their own admission. Adult anxiety sufferers are often reluctant to have relationships because at 50 they want to explore their "options" or start a family at 60. They are unable to see this as unrealistic or continually unfulfilling and the search for the "right one" continues into the end of life. Having dysfunctional finances and chaotic home lives are part of that immature unclear thinking in which they are unable to see their thinking and functioning are the root cause.

This appears interesting and fun in small increments to outsiders, but the anxiety sufferer is always on the verge of making it happen or making it good. A patient once said that for his entire life he just felt that it was always within his grasp yet he "could never grab it." The fact that it doesn't go as planned triggers the underlying depression that is fueling the anxiety in the first place.

Children with anxiety are often stuck in earlier stages, cry easily, and are attracted to toys, playmates, and ideas that are from the previous stage of development.

<u>Distortion</u> - It may appear that anxiety sufferers are liars or even delusional because they have a huge distortion of reality. Once an anxiety sufferer gets an idea in their mind, they cannot be convinced otherwise no matter what real evidence is presented. When disarmed they will change the subject as if it's a natural progression and rarely do they realize their fears

make no sense and are unfounded. When they do realize an unrealistic thought, they convince themselves that this is how everyone functions. Again, the racing thoughts prevent the person from hearing all that is being said in a simple conversation or exchange.

People with anxiety experience frequent altercations with others, especially those closest to them. Those who have generalized anxiety argue, accuse, persecute, and make judgmental demands on those in their lives on a regular and frequent basis. Ultimately those with anxiety suffer from depression but due to the chaotic nature of anxiety, depression is frequently difficult to see, determine, or feel.

Anxiety sufferers are often late, unnecessarily early, or never arrive because they were unable to control all the demands of getting from one place to another without the fear and self-inflicted chaos of their learned thinking.

Example: A woman who became a member of a group that met over appetizers called the group organizer after the third meeting and stated, "You don't have to make food if you don't want to, it's not necessary." That sentence sounds harmless, but an adult knows what they can and want to do, not to mention that there are other group members that don't share that thought. That statement was based on her own stuck ideas about what she wanted and needed to control.

By the fifth group meeting the woman phoned and wanted to change the time or not attend because she had been having dinner with her spouse on that same day for many years. She was unable to see that she did not have to eat the food at the meeting so she could eat dinner with her spouse or that she could miss one dinner with her spouse per month. People with anxiety get stuck on ideas or thoughts and then are unable to let go because they cannot control new circumstances and the racing thought makes it their truth.

Unawareness - The anxiety sufferer has the same thought racing day in and day out so when they are challenged on an issue and think they are losing control they feel attacked, rejected, and threatened. This results in an argument or conflict and can result in violence if two people are "dancing" for control. This is a similar feeling the person experienced as a child when the parental figure did not validate their feelings and took control in all situations.

One example of how this unawareness can be developed is when a parent came into my office and insisted that she has raised her eight-year-old to make her own decisions. Upon further exploration, I asked her how she helped her daughter make decisions and my patient responded by saying, "I ask her if she's sure." When we ask a child if they are sure, we are creating doubt and reducing self-esteem, which is the breeding ground for anxiety and depression.

They Suffer from Depression - There is NO anxiety without depression. You can have depression and not have anxiety but having anxiety means you have depression. Anxiety is the fire to the wood of depression. The anxiety is bold and is kept alive by being fed wood. If you try to put out the fire (anxiety) but keep giving it wood, then the fire which is anxiety will ignite. The challenge is getting an adult to see that their chaotic life is part of their depression and not their efforts (or lack of). One patient describes his depression as always having something just within his reach and yet not being able to ever reach it, no matter how hard he tried or what he did.

Young people need the help of someone with patience and empathy to learn that taking care of themselves is not an option. Gone are the days when you could eat, drink, live the life of a music video, and feel good and positive the next day. This is not going to happen in real life. It's important to understand that if that is how you have been living your life for most of your life, you would have to normalize this process. This is the dog-chasing-its-own-tail life process. My challenge is not curing anxiety; this is relatively easy compared to merely having an individual explore what depression looks like in them.

Anxiety is like a musical band. The band plays loudly each day, it's hard to focus, it's hard to hear full concepts from others, and in general, that band is in front of what is ultimately propelling the anxiety: depression. In my treatment, I know a person is getting better (anxiety disappearing) when they finally feel the depression. Depression is not felt when you have severe anxiety, but it is usually seen in behavior.

Another huge challenge is that depression is not accurately depicted or understood. It is not necessarily, nor is it usually, sadness. The life of someone with depression is lived in extremes and inappropriate emotions to life changes. In depression, you become "triggered" inappropriately. For example, you may have a situation in your life such as your best friend is deathly ill. If you have depression your emotions around this are at a 15 when the scale is 1 to 10. People with depression are off the chart in the severity of their emotions. This makes it almost impossible for treatment because they feel this is normal and some of it is accurate because, after all, their friend is sick. There is an actual situation, yet the circumstance doesn't warrant extreme emotion.

<u>Poor Decision Making</u> - Poor decision-making defines someone with anxiety and depression. The depressed individual believes they are just dealing with what is given. In the book *I Don't Want to Talk About It: Overcoming the Secret Legacy of Male Depression*, (Real, Terrence, 1997) Real writes that a great many men conceal their condition from the outside world and those close to them–loved ones, doctors, even psychotherapists–may miss a diagnosis of overt depression. They not only manage to camouflage their depression from those around them but hide it even from themselves.

They miss out on living fully and not just surviving because they don't have the clarity of thought to stand up for themselves and figure out what is really working for them. When you are depressed one huge trait is the lack of self-care. When we don't self-care (daily and conceptually) we are not taking care of anyone. Not ourselves or our loved ones (contrary to what we believe). Self-care is about doing what we say we want for ourselves and not blaming circumstances when it doesn't happen. It's ongoing and provides us with the framework to say no and set boundaries for things that don't work.

When anxiety and depression are felt (anxiety sufferers are good at suppressing feelings, this also makes them harmful) only then can the healing and care of self to others begin.

My patient Robert, age 52 (not his real name of course) has worked three jobs for as long as he can remember. In our first session, I confronted him with my assessment that he suffered from depression. He had some strong ideas about my judging him and insisting this is what he had to do for his family. I suggested Robert try a natural antidepressant just to see if he was able to even "hear" what both myself and his partner were stating. He complied after two months with the urging of his partner of 20 years and my persistence.

As we discussed what depression looked like, Robert began to realize he didn't have friends outside of work, only socialized with his partner, and only when she initiated events/outings. In fact, he only saw his family for small amounts of time and then he was exhausted and never fully enjoyed himself in any activity. Furthermore, he had allowed the family finances to become disorganized, which led him to have to continue to work three jobs. His normalized, yet chaotic, life bled into his intimacy with his partner and led to severe discord.

While on the natural antidepressant, Robert began to see things clearly in every aspect of his life. He quit two of his jobs, organized his finances, and is in the business of repairing the disconnected relationships with himself and his family. He verbalized to me that he had been in a "trance" for most of his life.

He cried for two 45-minute sessions. He then verbalized that he still had time and needed to move on from his regret of not seeing his depression earlier in life.

Anxiety Sufferers' Behavior and Thought Patterns are Degrading/Abusive

This concept is often difficult to both explain and to give examples. If each day of your life the people you look up to the most tell you that they hit, verbally degrade, or neglect you physically or emotionally because they love you, then abuse (degradation and abuse are one and the same) will seem normal. More importantly, you will grow up with those same thoughts about those that attempt to love you and about yourself.

My patient, we'll call him Luther, has three children (5, 9, and 12) whom after a breakup with his partner, he sees on most weekends. Luther and his children were invited to a rare all-inclusive weekend with a friend. He had not taken a vacation in four years. Luther just needed to provide transportation to the weekend vacation location. Unexpectedly Luther's car broke down (anxiety sufferers are frequently in chaos due to the constant negative unclear thinking) so he was provided a two-seater rental car. Not being able to take all his children Luther decided not to go at all. This is punishing behavior. Luther is punishing himself and at least one of his children. He verbalized that if they all could not attend then none of them should. It's abusive to not take care of yourself because if you do not take care of yourself, you cannot take care of others no matter what you think. This is also an example of backwards thinking. Without anxiety, he would have the ability to think of different ways to get some benefit out of the situation. Anxiety sufferers are frequently so stuck on a thought that they refuse to see differently or in a positive light.

Another example is a patient I'll call Ralph. Ralph (25 years old) had attracted a good-looking, intelligent woman who was kind and interested in him. Once Ralph began to get close (after three months) he decided that he should break off the relationship. When I asked him why, he reported that he might grow disinterested in her in the future. To Ralph, this was how life was supposed to work. Backwards thinking was how he learned to see situations. He was not aware of the fact that he was being abusive to both himself and to her. Ralph's anxiety dictated that he punish himself for having a good time in this relationship because the inevitable negative was pending.

Because people with anxiety attract others with anxiety, it is a challenge for the sufferer to understand that living in chaos (not having money, poor money management, daily living seems hectic, and life is frequently frantic) is not normal or necessary. Their belief is that everyone is like this, and they don't trust anyone who does not live in chaos and who is positive.

Severe anxiety sufferers are frequently fanatically religious (although they do not see themselves as such), or involved and working for paramilitary organizations (police, security, or related organizations). You will see them in any organization or program in which they are controlled or taught to control themselves or others. Anxiety sufferers have financial chaos often living beyond their means and then stressing over it or spending without a plan. This is how they have learned to function; they have gotten used to it as well as dysfunctional intimate relationships.

Most of the current violence by our young adults is based on the person having come from a home that has first taught the child that control is how life has to be conducted. That existence is almost impossible to survive, so the child has to disconnect from self and take on the thoughts and feelings of the parental figures' ideology no matter how backwards and abusive to the psychology. This is very difficult for us as a society to acknowledge let alone face.

As I write, we are in a much more triggered traumatic existence in our lives with the long-lasting effects of the Covid-19 pandemic than when I first began this book in 2015. It is far easier to see the anxiety and depression that is prevalent in our society. It's just now being talked about that we had a very high level of anxiety and depression in America and now our poor mental health is plaguing and dangerous. We still insist that just "talking" about depression and anxiety will help. We are told to just simply ask for "help." At this time, you will find it almost impossible to find a therapist in the United States because we have moved from our normal high anxiety to profoundly debilitating anxiety and depression. The question is how do we reset ourselves to our baseline or perhaps lower? I will address this in later chapters.

Anxiety is curable because it is learned. The real challenge is creating deliberate parents who are self-aware and have looked at how they were raised. We can no longer be afraid of discussing our poor parenting (that fear is steeped in anxiety) or the poor parenting of our parents. This will lead us to raise the expectations for ourselves and our children. If we begin to discuss how we raise children in a universal way, we can only then get to the root cause of the so-called random violence in our country.

My office is full of individuals who know they have anxiety and just can't live with it another day. Those are the people who are easily cured because they have managed to surrender enough to let a new idea in their minds and then get total relief. Young people come in just nervous, and they don't know why, or they have panic attacks and come with an open mind stating they will do "anything" not to have panic attacks.

On the other hand, anxiety is about control and so often individuals are not able to release control long enough to get help. They come to my office once and never return. As a person gets older, they become used to the anxiety and the pain and so find it comforting in a distorted kind of way, one patient described it as "a bad friend, but a familiar friend."

I describe anxiety as the inability to sustain a positive thought that manifests itself into a physical reaction that is constant. It never goes away and it can get worse. If having no anxiety is a 1 on a scale of 1 to 10, then anxiety sufferers live at a 5. This number may go much higher yet without treatment rarely lower. Stress is not anxiety. When you have an anxiety disorder your anxious thoughts are like a negative recording of being judged, being late, being too early, what will I say, I may fall, I may get sick, and the negative thoughts just go on and on and on. It is a miracle anxiety sufferers can function at all. This further exacerbates their depression and feelings of isolation.

Patricia Evans wrote a book entitled *Controlling People*. Ms. Evans did not realize that she was writing definition after definition of exactly what anxiety looks like, how it manifests, and how the anxiety sufferer thinks in great detail.

I will be using her book to guide us through the treatment and cure process.

Chapter 5

The Cure

We will be using three chapters of Patricia Evans' book *Controlling People*. Ms. Evans does an outstanding job, yet I want you to hold off on reading her book in its entirety at this time. As you work through the stages, resist your urge to read ahead. Take your time and allow yourself several weeks to think about and reread the stages. Moving quickly will hinder progress and ultimately hinder your success with this treatment.

Who This Cure May Not Work For

If an individual resides with their triggers, whether it is the parent or spouse (a parental figure), the cure will be a challenge to implement due to the constant negative reinforcement. For example, the parents of 10-year-old Louis brought him into my office for treatment of his severe anxiety. Louis had a fear of most things, and it was disturbing his school day and his daily living activities at home. I interviewed both parents to discover that mom yelled at him frequently and insisted that he was unable to function without her constantly verbally pushing him and her going behind him and completing his assigned at-home tasks. Dad (who was not in the home) reported he was an active church member and took Louis to church several times per week. Louis' only outside activity was karate.

Under those living conditions, Louis could not be treated effectively. The parents both would have to understand their anxiety, their role, and agree to be treated. It may sound obvious but when your child has an emotional problem the parent is usually the cause or at least has an incredible role in both the origin and the cure.

Oddly, most parents want to drop off their child so the therapist can fix them. What they usually want is for therapists to teach them how to be controlled by their parents. This is certainly not true when there are some organic issues. Anxiety is not organic. It is a learned behavior.

A second challenge would be a more severe mental illness. The treatment entails the cognitive and intellectual ability to verbalize and identify feelings. The intellect and ability to focus are needed to understand the history and cause of anxiety. This may be impossible if, for example, a patient suffers from schizophrenia or bipolar disorder. Although I have treated several bipolar or schizoid-trait patients who decreased their anxiety and made them more self-aware, it did not cure the anxiety disorder. These patients reported an increase in the quality of their lives, something that is beneficial no matter what our challenges.

The final caveat would be a chronic medical condition that causes chronic pain and discomfort. The basic premise of my treatment is getting you in touch with your physical feelings. Having pain caused by a medical condition would prevent the treatment process and physical pain can make it difficult to think positively (a key component in curing anxiety). That

The Cure

being said, the body is perfect, and frequently anxiety sufferers have a medical condition that their anxiety is causing. Whether it is heart problems, neck pain, back issues, or blindness, the mind will create fairly severe pain to get your attention to address your anxiety.

The majority of my practice consists of men and women from all races, cultures, and education under 45 years old, but I have had many successes with various ages. What I have seen and know is that an open mind is an open mind. If you open your mind and understand the power of a positive mind, then there is nothing you cannot do no matter what your age or state in life.

Before any treatment can make a difference, we must agree that your behavior and feelings of unhappiness and discomfort are caused by your anxiety. Those with anxiety yell at others, blame others for their unhappiness and experience constant and regular conflict with friends, neighbors, in business, and those closest to them. The turmoil also does not have to be overt. The conflicts with others can be kept inside and so to make sure that no one knows how backwards my thinking is, the anxiety sufferer will isolate as not to be judged or so that no one will see the "real me," the me that is negative and chaotic. This speaks a lot to what depression is and its role in anxiety.

The difficulty for the anxious person is to understand that most people do not argue, hate life, or walk around with negative thoughts. It must be brought to their attention that people are satisfied with their lives and even happy for the most part.

Anxiety: Curing the New Normal

The anxious person has learned to live with the misery of their anxiety and believes that everyone has anxiety and that people are just generally not happy. They learn to manage their anxiety and may have spent a great deal of time learning that management. Believe it or not, this is my most challenging task. The anxious person often attributes their anxiety as part of their "character." They have lived with it for so long that it's like an old friend. It's an awful friend, but it's still a friend! Of course, the reality is that anxiety is based on fear and control, so losing anything is a problem for the anxious person.

In therapy, this is called resistance. It can last for many months or take as little as a few weeks to break the resistance and have an agreement. Once we come to that agreement, I find the patient has some relief. They often say they feel better just letting go of one fear (one of their biggest). This can provide relief, but the journey will get worse before it gets better.

I use several tools to educate those with anxiety about how a power struggle in their youth resulted in their feeling fearful of everything around them and therefore needing to feel in control. They were controlled as children to the extent that they had no identity and never learned to make a mistake, correct it, and feel good about that process.

People with anxiety grew up with verbally, emotionally or physically controlling and abusive parental figures. Although we as individuals have a general understanding of psychology, somehow when I present that our parents are responsible for our thinking and how we function as adults this is often hard to comprehend and frequently the more severe the abuse the more difficult for the adult child to acknowledge.

Sometimes we know our parents were not there for us or ridiculed us and it's too painful to go over. The other issue with seeing the role of your parents in your pathology is that it may not be clear to you because you don't know any better. How would a child see that how they were being treated was not healthy? The parents are seen as all-knowing and no matter how the child feels about what is being done, they have no choice but to accept their plight in life. The child wants the parent to know all the answers. It makes the child feel secure. I frequently have very intelligent patients who report that they knew their parents had issues and "were crazy" but they had to survive. What is a five-year-old to do? Pack their bags and move out? No, the child wanted to believe that the parents loved them, to teach and define what love looks like.

I had a patient who revealed that in her childhood her mom burned her, yet she came to feel that was okay because the mother was under stress with the other four children. How do we know what is bad behavior from a parent when they seem to love us, and we desperately want that love? Learned behavior is just that; learned. We normalize what is not healthy in order to survive. It is difficult to see the dysfunction and its impact when you have only one experience and nothing else. This is the biggest problem because we simply repeat it on our own children and unknowingly on ourselves. It was only when my patient's mother began to verbally abuse her daughter that my patient confronted the mother and set very strong boundaries.

To raise a healthy, happy person, a parental figure would have to praise the child each day for all things, not just when they work out. The job is to teach them to figure out how to think and feel about the consequences and decisions of daily life. The parent would have to hold a positive thought about the process of raising a child into adulthood and have that goal in the very fiber of their existence each day. Studies show that to have a happy child you must have a happy parent.

This example is a similar one from *Controlling People* (P. Evans): a child walks into an ice cream store with the parent and says, "I want strawberry ice cream." The parent says, "You hate strawberry ice cream so get chocolate." The child says, "No I want strawberry." The parent says, "I know what you like," and tells the clerk to give the child chocolate ice cream.

This is teaching the child:

- That others know how you think and feel better than you do.

- Disconnect from your own thoughts and feelings in order to think the way others want you to.

- You are not capable of making or knowing how you think or feel.

The scenario should have gone like this: When the child says, "I want strawberry," the parent says,

The Cure

"Okay last week you didn't like strawberry but in life, smart people try new things." I had a patient tell me that choosing the wrong ice cream would result in a financial loss for the parent. That may be true but it's also a thought based on fear. Not to mention that teaching lessons to a child is expensive in many ways. Not just financially. One very young and bright patient stated that the whole scenario sounded premeditated and abusive, "If you are going to choose, why not get a carton of ice cream from the store when you are alone and bring it home." The unobstructed mind is more powerful than we can begin to understand.

This is where we begin to retrain the brain. What can I say about this that won't sound crazy or over the top? Years ago, I read about a therapist who would "suggest" to his patients about feeling better and they started feeling better. It sounded good to me, so I did some reading and experimenting when I was just starting my career and got positive results. Since that time, I have used it in my treatment of anxiety and really, it's what all good therapists do. I tell you you are going to get better; I know that you will, and you do. If it sounds hokey think about the fact that if you had a child and each day from its youth you told him or her, they were smart and you actually BELIEVED it (and backed that up with proof), do you think that by the time they became adults, they would eventually be smart?

What is key to this is consistency. My hypnotherapy is done with my voice. I am confident in my voice and at the same time repetitive in my words and the tone of my voice. Having had years of success also helps. I tell my patients that this will work because it has in the past. It's that simple. We are in fact focusing on the truth in the moment.

There are some elements to this portion of the treatment that are mindfulness-based. This is not a minor idea. It will be the foundation of the treatment and responsible for creating lasting happiness.

Positive thinking is not the opposite of negative thinking. It's a stand-alone thought about this moment.

We give the feelings names and begin to teach easy parenting techniques or communication skills in couples. Those not in relationships begin to explore themselves and their role in adding to or helping the world without fear. Depending on the age of the patient there is usually some degree of depression because the feelings had never been validated throughout childhood. The depression at this point is very easy to see and because the individual is now in touch with their feelings of depression it is addressed with greater ease.

After the age of 32 years (based on my experience) anxiety will not be stabilized unless the depression is acknowledged and a long-term treatment plan for depression is devised.

I think about depression like type 2 diabetes. If you eat properly, keep your weight down, and exercise, you can live a full and long life with diabetes. There are several levels of diabetes and your mature commitment to taking care of yourself is everything. The same is true for depression.

My patient, who initially arrived resistant to taking anything for depression, described depression as a train. "A train that has many stops. You can get off at the first stop or the last stop, it's up to you but you will get off." Very well stated because depression is progressive, and the symptoms of anxiety are so varied that we normalize them and thereby risk our entire quality of life.

The American Psychological Association reports that individuals who suffer from depression are 70% more likely to suffer an untimely death. This is due to poor self-care and unclear thinking that describes depression.

Antidepressants have drastically changed in the last 10 years. We know so much more and can agree that a person who suffers from depression can live a stable life without issues.

Depression stabilization should be looked at the same way we need to look at ourselves each year as we age. It is about learning how to take care of yourself to do more and be more here on this planet, if not for ourselves, then for others that we love, or those who need our strength, insight, and intelligence. This is no small task I realize, but it can be done, and once able to see clearly the depressed individual has the insight and energy to do what each of us should do to sustain our health and wellness.

Patients get permission to let go of doing the same thing that is not working. At this stage, most see what is needed and identify patterns easily. The patient lets go because holding on is a negative thought and negative thinking was addressed.

Because the psychic boundaries of the anxiety-afflicted patient were infringed upon their entire life (abuse says you don't matter and so this must be how the world operates) we have to define boundaries in all that they do. In a short time, this becomes instinctive.

Chapter 6

The Treatment

I will need you to read three chapters from Patricia Evans' book *Controlling People*. We are only going to use three chapters. You are free to obtain and read the entire book at some other point after you have completed this anxiety cure process.

Please read the chapter "The Problem" two to three times before moving to the next step. You will be asked a series of questions after each page. Please take notes and take your time to reflect after reading each page. Once you begin, I need you to take three to four weeks before you move on to the next stage.

Anxiety is progressive so just like cancer it can and will get worse without treatment. The anxiety you feel today will not remain the same in a year from now or five years from now. When a 25-year-old comes into my office I explain to them that their anxiety will increase and as miserable as they feel today, they have yet to experience the extent of the pain anxiety causes.

I want to say a word about this treatment and age. I have realized that although it can appear to be easier to treat and cure a 25-year-old than a 45-year-old, the reason for that is not so obvious. First, an older anxiety sufferer eliminates anyone and anything that they deem as causing them anxiety (that could be the entire world) but what that does in treatment is make them isolated. (Isolation is also a sign of depression).

It then becomes difficult to find examples to use in the treatment of their backwards thinking. To the older sufferer, if they have eliminated everyone around them, they have normalized their isolation. The older anxiety sufferer has also developed many "tricks" that they believe are helping them "manage" their anxiety and the reality is that the "tricks" are both adding on a complication and exacerbating the cause of the anxiety. It has been brought to my attention by my older patients that age ultimately doesn't matter as the brain doesn't know how old it is. If you are open to learning and can stay focused, you can learn something new at any age.

Stage 1

How Did I Get Anxiety?

So, by now you should have read the chapter "The Problem" at least two or three times. Let's begin with the first page, page 10.[3]

Patricia Evans tells the story of Nan. If we look at page 10 (the third paragraph) she writes, "While she was growing up the people who were responsible for her had acted senselessly against her–people who were old enough to know better–people who thought that they *were* sensible. They had disparaged her, ridiculed her, and thus defined her. They had oppressed her and attempted to control her. The people who treated her this way were in fact her parents."

So, this is how it works; you have a parent and a child. They are in the ice cream store when the child says to the parent, "Today I'm going to try bubble gum ice cream."

The parent says, "Well, you always get chocolate ice cream. I know you are going to get the chocolate, just go ahead and get the chocolate."

The child says, "Today I want to try something new. I want to try the bubble gum ice cream. That blue looks interesting, I like how the bubblegum looks."

And the parent says to the child, "You're probably not going to like it and you're going to throw it out so just get the chocolate." At that point, the parent turns

---

[3] Evans, Patricia. *Controlling People*. Adams Media, 2002.

to the clerk and says they'll (the child) have the chocolate. That parent's behavior teaches three things.

The first thing that teaches is that the child is stupid (this is how the child will ultimately feel and internalize those words). I'm telling my child that he/she's stupid because they are not able to make their own decisions. They don't know what they want, or they don't know what they like. The job of the parental figure is to teach a child how to think, not think for them. A child comes with some natural instincts that are to be nurtured through exploration. But the average parent doesn't want that job, it's too much talking and thinking, and that nature stuff is ridiculous, it just makes children disrespectful and unruly. "I want to do what was done to me, even though it was harsh and hurt me. Ima do what my parents did."

The second thing that it teaches the child is that this is how relationships function; you're going to have people tell you how to think and feel and you are just going to sit there and wait until people tell you how to think and feel whether you're seven, 10, 15 or 30 years old. So the seven-year-old goes on the playground and here comes the bully (there's no such thing as bullying). The "bully" punches him and says "Hey, give me your lunch money and open that bag and give me any snacks you have."

The child says, "Okay, okay. I just want you to be nice to me. I just want you to like me."

The bully says, "Well, you better bring me your lunch money every single day."

The child thinks, *Okay I know how this works. This is how it works at home, too. I have to do things to make my parents like me and to accept me and to love me so I'm familiar with this. I just want you to like me and so I know you will love me only if I do exactly what you say.* The bully punches the child and walks away.

So, there is no victim or perpetrator, only the dance learned in childhood. They are really both victims of poor and abusive parenting. Then the child grows up to be 15 and he's online at his computer or he has his phone and he's on social media and people are telling him you should kill yourself you're so stupid you're so ugly and the child says maybe I am, there's something wrong with me that's true. I have to listen to other people. It's true they define me.

Social media says, "Why are you wearing that, why do you look like you're not doing enough, if you talk to that person we're not going to be friends with you." When that same child gets to be 20 years old and in a relationship, the dance of the relationship goes like this: "Who are you talking to? Let me see your phone! Where are you going? Where were you? I need to be in control of you, you can't go there, you have to come here, do this, do that. The child gets to be an adult and marries that, and then raises their children in that same controlling pattern. This is how the child begins to believe that this is what relationships look like; people tell me how to think and feel and therefore probably I'm supposed to tell them also how they think and feel.

The third thing that it teaches the child is that you don't really have feelings. Yet, we all come with a set of feelings and intuition just a little bit when you first arrived here. You see, you have the same heart and the same lungs on the day you were born as you have right now. And you have the same heart and the same lungs until the day you die. So, you come with natural circumstances but if you're not allowed to express those and have them validated, then what you do is suppress your own thoughts and feelings and take on the thoughts and feelings of others. This breeds depression. The child has to suppress themselves so that they can ensure being loved.

As we continue on the bottom of page 10, we see that at age 19, a very young age, Nan moved away from home and moved in with a new-found partner. She writes in that last paragraph at the bottom of page 10, "She met a charming and intelligent man but upon marrying him, he changed drastically."

But did he change drastically? No, of course, he did not change. She just was not able to see it or more importantly she did see it and she was attracted to those dynamics of control and abuse. Why? Because she was used to it from her childhood. She had married into the kind of relationship that she had with her parents. Very controlling, very abusive, very invalidating.

If Nan was to meet someone that was validating and they stood next to her, the signaling in her body would give off the feeling that there was nothing going on, no excitement, a weird kinda peace, and boredom. If there was a peace within that person; that person didn't live in chaos and didn't degrade her, she would have thought that that inner peace was actually something negative. She was not accustomed to having peace (no physical signaling in the body). So, Nan is attracted to what she's accustomed to which is chaos, invalidation, degradation, and abuse and that is what she married.

I want you to think about the aspects of your life that you can relate to with men or women who are abusive in your life, now or in the past. Are you able to see patterns in your life that your parents were invalidating?

Reflect on page 10 and write your thoughts below.

The Treatment

Let's look at page 11. As we move through these three chapters of Patricia Evans' book *Controlling People,* we will be using several concepts and vocabulary words. Two of those concepts are self-esteem and positive thinking.[4] She writes in the second paragraph on page 11, "Whole Industries are built around raising self-esteem and developing positive thinking." We are going to really look at how we raise our self-esteem. This self-esteem should have been developed in childhood. Because you have anxiety and depression, we can tell that this self-esteem did not develop. We will look at how we reinvent ourselves. That is self-actualization and we will be working with that concept in great detail.

The other part is positive thinking. What is positive thinking? Positive thinking is not used as a trend word. We will look at positive thinking as an actual real concept and idea that we will pick away at, fully develop and fully understand in a way that puts us here in the moment. Able to see joy from moment to moment. I want you to look at this page and see what you can take away and relate to your own life now and in the past.

Next, let's look at the concept of covert and overt control in interpersonal relationships. Evans explains that "in personal relationships, many people have experienced inexplicable acts against them that are covert or overt attempts to control them."[5] Overt control is when you constantly tell a person what to do and everything negative about what they do and what

---

[4] See *Controlling People (2002),* p. 11.
[5] Ibid, p. 11.

they don't do. So that would be the mother with the child yelling at a child constantly telling them, "Stop, don't do this, stop that, say this, don't say that." This type of control is very obvious. Of course, the controller doesn't see this as controlling and is often not even raising their voice.

Covert control is a little different as covert control would look like a child who gets whatever they want from parents. This tells the child that you are not capable of being independent. You are not smart and cannot take care of yourself. You need others to get your needs met and always will.

As your parent demonstrating covert control, I pretend that I am being "nice" when in fact I want you to like and love me, so I am controlling your point of view of me. They are telling the child that the child is not entitled to their own thoughts and their own feelings and use this as a way to control into adulthood. The deliberate parent, that is to say, a parent who understands a little bit about child development and their role as a "master teacher" and not a "master punisher," would certainly help the child express their thoughts and their feelings in a way that is appropriate but also validating and helps them negotiate getting what they want at five years old and then through life.

In interpersonal relationships one partner tells the other what they want to hear. This is done so that you will stay in relationship with them. As a person expressing covert control, I am again attempting to control your feelings about me like I was taught in childhood. The fact is that if I then show you my real feelings, then you are not going to like the real me, so

The Treatment

I have to control that outcome. The truth is that we want people around us who see us and love us for who we really are, not who they think we should be or who they want us to be. But if your parent didn't listen or hear your thoughts, feelings, and ideas, then you were left to think they are not important. Only all external (outside of me and myself) ideas, concepts, and people matter.

Another example of covert control can look like a partner going on a diet and the other partner bringing inappropriate food into the home all the while saying, "This is just for me you don't have to eat this." What they are really doing is making sure that the partner doesn't change. The change means that they might be left if their partner gets healthy, fit, and trimmer. This could also mean that they feel they might also have to be healthy, trimmer, and fit. Once one aspect changes in a relationship, further change is imminent.

In young adulthood that covert control looks like a parent sharing adult thoughts and feelings to keep the child fearful of going out on their own. For example, a parent might say "Oh, I feel terrible I want to kill myself," or "my life is awful." They may talk to the child about all the issues (negative thinking) that they have to go through in life. That would then somehow and frequently does make the young adult adolescent feel they are responsible for the emotional well-being of the parent. That's what the parent had been taught in their childhood and therefore their child (now the young adult) will not be able to go out on their own and take care of themselves. They are being trained to be beholden to the parent and feel guilty well into adulthood.

An example of very covert control is when a young adult cannot do something as natural as leaving home to find independence. Frequently young people are unable to finish college or even leave home because they do not have the self-esteem or the positive thinking that is needed to establish confidence in their youth.

Reflect by writing your ideas and questions on the above.

Anxiety: Curing the New Normal

At the bottom of page 11, we read the italicized story. The father who was abused turned into an abuser and was not able to see this. If we could wish away our abusive, chaotic childhoods simply, the world would be perfect. Just saying I won't treat my child the way I was treated does not and will not work. This is important because as you move through this process of coming out of anxiety, it is very important that you understand that you have surrounded yourself with people who also have anxiety. It is comfortable and it is all that you know.

In a short time, you will not be able to tell them and explain to them simply and easily that they have backwards thinking and that how they are thinking is inappropriate and their behavior is also inappropriate. We learn things from childhood and that childhood is cemented like a brick into our psychology and it cannot be changed so easily. What we are doing is chipping away at it with a very fine chisel and we are chipping at dust until eventually the dust turns into smaller particles, the particles turned into larger rocks until eventually that cemented block of how you were raised with backwards thinking both fall away naturally.

Bear in mind that it is not so easy to change what we learned from childhood. I had a patient, a very small, lovely young woman of twenty years old, tell me that she was a terrible person, so she could relate to page 12. I thought about that as my first instinct was to rescue her, yet I asked why she felt that way. She stated she was a terrible person because "frequently I do not respond to text messages from my friends." She further reported that she stands them up, she is three hours late, she says yes when she wants to say no, she ghosts those she can't confront or who can't confront her.

My response to her was it was unfortunate she had horrible parents and so she never stood a chance. If she was never taught that she could say no to some things in her life, then she now understands that she has to say yes to everything in order to control how others think and feel about her. This is similar to her childhood in which she had to listen and go along in order to get love from her parents. She verbalized to me that when she is looking down on herself at her bad behavior, she feels like she is a terrible person, but she is unable to stop it. She is a dog chasing his tail. She feels bad that she is not a good friend, and this makes her depressed and her being depressed further makes her not a good friend.

As we retrain the brain, we will understand that we have a right to all of our thoughts and all of our feelings at all times and that we are only looking for the people who want and accept us. And the rest will just drop away naturally as we attach ourselves to more and more positive people who accept us for who we are.

Please reflect in writing.

The Treatment

On page 13, let's look at the italicized story as the gentleman talks about his dysfunctional relationship with his wife. Ms. Evans quotes one of her clients as saying, "No one witnessed it because I was nice and kind to our friends. But when no one was around I got very irrational and angry." The dynamic of that is simply that when you have anxiety, and you are out in the world you have to make everybody like and love you, so you have to control how they think and feel about you. You accomplish this by doing things that you deem as "nice" and that you think they want you to do or want you to say. When you come home like a hamster on a wheel, you are no longer the controlled, you are the controller. The child learned in childhood that the elements of control and chaos must be present or there is no relationship, no love. The parents said, "I love you," "I am doing this for your own good," and "I know what is best for you," as they degraded, controlled, and abused the child by not validating his/her feelings, wants and ultimately her/his individual needs as a person.

I use the analogy of two hamsters on a wheel: it appears as though the hamsters are chasing one another. First picture one hamster on a wheel spinning round and round and he is going no place. That is the state of having anxiety; you are moving fast, and it looks like you are doing something but ultimately, you're going nowhere and doing nothing. When you add another hamster on that wheel and the wheel spins both ways it looks as though one is chasing the other, but the fact of the matter is they are only about control and that hamster wheel will never end up in

Europe or Africa no matter how long or how fast they move on that wheel.

That's a great analogy for the dance of two people vying for control doing what they learned in childhood. At any given time, each hamster can change positions and the other appears to be chasing (or controlling the other) this is not the case. There is no victim. That behavior described on 13 is punishing.[6] The punishing behavior of not speaking to a partner or friend is ultimately saying, "I'm ahead of you" and "I'm above you and so this is your punishment you don't get to speak to me the almighty/the all-knowing."

That again was learned in childhood in which the parent was overpowering the child and saw the child as less than and that in order for me to get you to do what I want you to do I'm going to need to constantly punish, degrade, and abuse you. All of this is exactly the opposite of how relationships function. That is what we call backwards thinking.

You are not a victim. Understand that we give our power away. Women frequently do this when they try to save their dysfunctional partner and even more so when we don't see that we are dysfunctional and remain in dysfunction despite obvious evidence. We must have standards; this is in no way referring to children or anyone who is not able to intellectually sense what is harmful to them in their personal lives.

Anxious relationships are dysfunctional, they are dysfunctional because the child has learned that there is no relationship without dysfunction, chaos, and

---

[6] Ibid, p. 13.

The Treatment

control and they repeat this in their adult relationships. That is what is comfortable when you have anxiety and so you "call" that to you, you are attracted to it. Having inner peace, being centered is something that's not recognizable, in fact it's something that feels uncomfortable. Whether it shows up as illness, arguments, an unclear life path, or dysfunctional interpersonal relationships, when you suffer from anxiety you find comfort in chaos, real or imagined.

As we look on the bottom of page 14, Evans discusses the picture being complete. The smallest pieces fit. Nothing I hope is overlooked. What we must understand is that if we continue to look at things in a very primitive way, we are piecing together behavior that cannot make sense unless we look at the big picture. The big picture is the pathology and the childhood in which the pathology originated. This speaks to the normalizing of how hard your life is, why things are "not working out." If you are normalizing your unhappiness you're not asking and looking at yourself in a larger conceptual, meaningful way.

Reflect in writing.

The Treatment

Once upon a time there was a skunk and he was living his life using his natural ability to squirt this very strong smell, yet those around him were telling him that he was too stinky. On social media, people were saying things like, "We can't hang around you, we don't want to speak to you, you have a bad smell, you've got to get rid of that smell, you just have got to do something about that or we're never going to speak to you."

So, he goes home one day, and he asks his skunk parents to give him $6,000 so that he can get his skunk gland removed, and being the invalidating, abusive, detached skunk parents they were, they said yes. So off he goes and finds a skunk surgeon who takes his $6,000 and removes the skunk gland and now what? Now he's looking behind every door behind his back constantly because he has nothing that can keep him safe.

What he did is what we do: we remove what was supposed to keep us safe, alert, aware, and centered. He thought it was a negative just like we do. We think that every time we have a feeling it is immediately interpreted as negative when in fact it is there to help us remain aware. It is not necessarily a negative at all. The key is to interpret these feelings correctly.

Use this time to reflect and take notes on how you are perhaps listening to others and not asking why you feel the way you feel.

The Treatment

On page 15 we are basically looking at the fact that it gets very easy to get sidetracked in the details of life.[7] You constantly may feel like it is the other person, or it is a set of circumstances that you're in that you cannot get out from under. You may feel like you are drowning and that any day now this is going to get better except the years are passing by. We have to understand the big picture: you are just reliving how your parents treated you day in and day out, and you are walking around with every negative word your parents had for you.

Today what we are doing is we are **reinventing self**. We are retraining the brain to think, we are chipping away at the ideas that were cemented in the brain during childhood. This is not an easy task because that cement block is very, very strong, and anything that we learned in childhood we take on as absolute truth. But the process is that we chip away at that cement block first until that block eventually falls away. At that time, you create a self-actualized self. The self that you want to be, that you understand your thoughts and your feelings, and you are defined solely by what you think and what you feel, not anyone else.

When I first read Patricia Evans' book and this particular chapter, having heinous acts against children and random acts of violence were fairly rare. At this time, although it is very commonplace, we are still not able to look at our role in it and the root cause of negative thinking and violence. Evans talks about

---

[7] Ibid, p. 15.

the Timothy McVeigh situation in 1995.[8] We can imagine and understand the kind of parenting that Timothy McVeigh encountered in order for him to see that the ultimate control was to kill, to murder people, and ultimately innocent children. This is still what we see regularly. On a smaller scale, we see this in our interpersonal relationships.

When we talk about being treated as an object or when we talk about not validating a child, ultimately you are saying you don't have any thoughts and feelings, you are not entitled to any thoughts or feeling, this is the basic description of an object. Objectification then bleeds into every day of your life. You don't see yourself as a person and you don't see others as people. They can come and go. I can take them or leave them. Therefore, it is very easy to hurt them and to hurt yourself as well. An object feels nothing, but a child, fortunately, holds on to all of his or her experiences whether he holds onto them emotionally or physically. That is a very important part of what we will be working on.

---

[8] Ibid, p.16.

The Treatment

Write thoughts and feelings.

At the bottom of page 16, Evans writes destructive acts such as striking a child to get it to stop crying. Such acts against children destroy their ability to release their emotions, confuse them, and leave them with buried rage. When you have anxiety you really have two emotions: one is angry, and the other is not angry. The fact of the matter is that most emotions are in the gray; the gray area we are going to learn to live in and exist there and this is what most of life is about. Everything is not perfect, but everything is also not negative.

There are a plethora of emotions that when you have anxiety you are not aware of because you were not given the opportunity to learn about emotions and feelings when you were a child. You were simply taught and told how to think and feel. Ultimately, negative thinking that is anxiety leads to violence. It has to be because all pathology is progressive. Just like cancer left untreated, what happens? Yes, it gets worse.

Progressive anxiety (and depression) either lead to physical violence against others or violence against self, which includes self-destructive behaviors or suicide. While it may be easy to spot terrorism in other cultures, sometimes we may not recognize the terrorism close to home. Are you terrorizing your children, partner, coworkers, or staff?

We continue to think that other circumstances are the root of our destruction. This is not to say that bad things don't happen in life, but this is rare when you talk about day-to-day living. People that have anxiety live in constant pain and chaos to the extent that to survive it they suppress it and eventually further lose awareness through disconnection the older they become.

Anxiety: Curing the New Normal

Write your thoughts and feelings.

The Treatment

Page 17 is extremely important, and Ms. Evans does an outstanding job of describing something that is very difficult to put into words. Specifically, we are looking at words and concepts that she uses, and we will use them over and over again. One of the concepts again is ***backwards thinking***. We were taught in a backwards way to not listen to ourselves, our physical feelings and what nature gave us; our emotions and intuition. On the middle of page 17 number one we will substitute the word perpetrators for controllers.

1. Controllers "usually believe that their oppressive actions are necessary, even right. Their behavior is actually the opposite, unnecessary and wrong." That means that when you have a negative thought it grows. It may start out as a small idea and maybe a criticism but because thinking grows it then turns into something that's absolutely negative and horrific.

The brain can also promote a positive thought. It is the same brain and the same energy so the same way that you can have a negative thought and allow it to grow, you can have a positive thought and allow it to grow. It starts out as something very small and grows into something very big and negative. For example, you may be having a conversation and there may be something that is brought up that is negative and at the end of the conversation you have convinced yourself that you hate yourself and you hate the other person and everything wrong in between. This of course is not accurate. When you have anxiety you constantly ruminate so are not able to hear the complete story and what you do hear is filtered through depressed negative thinking.

2. "Generally, acts against others, that is, attempts to control others, eventually bring the perpetrators just the opposite of what they want." This is true especially in parenting and also in your interpersonal relationships. We cannot raise a child with unhappiness and fear and expect them to grow up and have positive, happy friends when they are five, a validating, positive girlfriend when they are 15 or a healthy relationship with a long-term partner when they are 30 years old. If the parenting style was one of fear and invalidation that is how the child will see life.

It is said that happy people raise happy children. That is the simplified way of stating that you should not expect to have a happy functional child if you are not happy and functional as a parent. This takes a lot of honesty and self-reflection, but there is a lot at stake. When we are raising children, it is not about us or even the one child. Perhaps it is about our legacy, the fact that hundreds and thousands will come after us when we are long gone. We have choices to make in our parenting. The choices are: do we look at ourselves in a harsh way because there is so much at stake or do we just continue to do what our parents did to us?

Each day parents bring their children in to me after having been a very strict parent, especially concerning their studies. Unfortunately, due to this unnecessary strictness their child cannot complete school because they have such profound negative thinking and racing thoughts that they are unable to think. Again, that gave the parents the exact opposite of what they say that they wanted. We have to understand that people are people, not objects and they have to have their emotional lives addressed first and foremost.

3. "Acts against others originate with a distortion or lack of awareness." Those two concepts are extremely important, and we will be using them repeatedly. "Perpetrators almost universally believe that they see clearly and are aware, the *opposite* of reality." Distortion is about that backwards thinking and if we look at how that happens, we can use a record player as an analogy. That LP is playing on the record player, and it gets a scratch in the groove of the album. We can walk away and return days later, and that scratched album will still be playing repeatedly when we return. You have to manually push that needle off the scratched album but, in the meantime, it has played over and over again. That is how it works in the mind of someone with anxiety. You play the same track in your mind repeatedly and so when you are presented with the facts, all you know is what your mind tells you. It is stuck and it cannot be changed.

Frequently when you have a conversation with someone with anxiety, they will say random things that have nothing to do with what you are discussing. This is due to the fact that this racing thought has to get out of their mind, and they are struggling to figure out a way to let it go. Again, because the thought is negative, it may start out as a little negative, but negative thoughts grow. So, the thought is negative, it grows into something more intensely negative and so it is not a little wrong, it is the exact opposite of the reality of the situation. Also, keep in mind that when you are on that track, that looping thought process, you are unable to hear situations and people clearly and fully, so you may come across as a liar because you are not in the moment fully at any given time.

Looking at this, you need to ask yourself, *What do you see? Do you see your life in this description? Do you relate to this? What has occurred in your life with your parents that have caused you to have negative thinking?* The other difficult question is to look at your parenting style (past, present, or future). Is it that slave parenting style that is an invalidating parenting style?

Recall how we talked about overt and covert control and my example of allowing the child to do whatever they would like to do (limit setting is gray not black or white). This creates a child that doesn't understand boundaries. We will discuss a great deal about boundaries. Understanding the importance of boundaries is critical because without boundaries we repeat our childhood wound of being an object. Even though this happened to you as an adult, you do not need to play the victim role any longer. Your behavior is learned from childhood and certainly I am not talking about children. I am talking about adults who can now look at things objectively and understand what is good for them and what is not good for them especially when it is blatantly abusive and unhealthy. This is a challenge I do understand, but there is no difference between a man and a woman when it comes to being invalidated in childhood. We all must take responsibility for ourselves and our children in seeing the patterns of abuse and invalidation.

Journal on thoughts and feelings below.

Evans gives the example of a couple that used conflict as a way to control one another.[9] After twenty years of harsh treatment, the wife moved out.

"Her husband always wanted her back and even after two years hoped she would return . . . He said, 'She just wants me to be nice to her.'

'Is it possible that you could be nice to her?' I asked.

'How can I be nice to her when I'm so angry that she left?'"

Again, we talked about being stuck on negative emotions because the person has not learned the gray of emotions and feelings in childhood, so again it is either angry or not angry, black or white. In childhood, the parent taught the child they (and then as an adult other adults) would dictate their emotions and that left the child with buried rage which means they are unable to verbalize their thoughts and feelings.

I have couples that come in and one partner does not talk, and the other partner is furious because they feel like their partner is just not talking to them because they are not attached to them or they just don't want to. The reality is that they do not know how to talk and when they do finally say something, they are accustomed to being ridiculed, invalidated, and objectified. This would then lead them to again not say anything, further lessening their ability to learn the vocabulary of their emotions. The problem with being stuck on the album is that it didn't just get stuck one day. It was stuck when the child was five years old, 10 years old for one month, it was stuck on a

---

[9] Ibid, p. 18.

thought when the person was 15 years old, stuck on a thought for six months when they were 20, and on and on. Those months add up to years of not allowing additional information into the brain that would mature the person.

This causes anxiety sufferers to be extremely immature, frequently unable to understand their emotions or how life works fully and without boundaries. An example of that would be a patient who got married when he was 35 years old with the understanding that everything would just be perfect. However, he questioned why it had to be so much work and why he had to negotiate continually with his partner. This is again immature thinking from being stuck on ideas for months and years at a time.

Journal on thoughts and feelings.

The Treatment

Evans writes, "Since all oppressive acts have a backwards quality to them they can be said to take place in the context of backwardness."[10] So again, understanding that the thinking is backwards is like living in a world of individuals who are walking backwards. They are falling over things, they are tripping off of curbs, they are constantly getting hurt but they think, *If everybody else is doing it, it must be normal. Even though there is blood running down my leg and I spend a lot of time in pain and it's difficult to get around as my wounds heal, I am not able to understand why I should walk forward and not backwards. It was taught to me in my childhood and if I go against my parents then perhaps, they will not love me. They may even be deceased or elderly, but I still cannot go against the ideas that they taught me because somehow, I am still striving to win their love. Perhaps if I do enough, say enough, be enough they will find a way to love me.*

Again, this is very backwards thinking no matter what the role others have in our lives. In the one life that we have we must be able to understand that we are looking for a few people who see us for exactly who we are, not who they want us to be. This ultimately prevents us from having people in our lives who just see us and accept us for exactly who we are. When you have anxiety, you spend most of your time on people that are not there sincerely for you. They are there because of who you present yourself to be. When we present ourselves as exactly who we are we have real intimacy, and we have true relationships. Allow those people to drop away who are not meant

---

[10] Ibid, p. 19.

for you and allow the people who are meant exactly for you to come to the forefront. In this way, you will find inner peace by calling the positive to you each and every day.

Finally, at the bottom of page 19, Ms. Evans writes "even ordinary behaviors are inexplicable unless we are aware of the context in which they take place. Once we understand the context, we can begin to interpret the behaviors and most importantly, to find out why the context of backwardness exists."

We have looked at why it does exist, we will move forward in understanding exactly how it was created inside the body and inside the mind and how we heal that. We cannot get stuck on individual stories of day-to-day living and how people are struggling. We have to look at the big picture of our role in our dysfunction and the role of our childhoods.

Stage 2

Sitting With Self

The Beginning of Mindfulness Simplified

At this stage, stage 2, we are looking at chapter six, "Disconnection: Training, Trying, and Trauma." Turn to page 40 and read the top paragraph. Please read the following paragraph twice before proceeding.

Ms. Evans writes, "We weigh our feelings, attend to our intuitive sense of the situation at hand, and note the sensations our body reveals. In fact, because our feelings, intuition, and sensations give us knowledge that we actually experience, they are our primary sources of information."

This means that we weigh our feelings from moment to moment at any given time, and we are in touch with what we're feeling through the body. "Attend to our intuitive sense of the situation at hand," means that we have a sense of intuition about any given moment, any given circumstance. This intuition is how our mind and our body work together to process information. "Note the sensation our body reveals," means that we feel it inside our body when things are going on. "In fact, because our feelings, intuition and sensations give us knowledge" means that we can figure out what is going on all around us through noting our mind and body and our intuition. "That we actually experience, they are our primary sources of information" means that we thought for the longest time that it was about our thinking, but we now understand that our thinking is backwards, so we are now going inside the body to feel our physical feelings.

So, this is what I need you to do: I need you to actually feel your physical feelings from moment to moment. That requires that you're not going to analyze what's going on. I am not referring to your thoughts or feelings or emotions. I am only referring to physical feelings inside the body at any given time.

For one week, you're going to simply document what you have felt physically. For example, if you're standing in front of me and I put my finger on your knee, I want you to just be able to experience what that feels like and then come back and describe it. Again, you're not going into your head to analyze, you are staying inside the body and feeling what that feels like. For example, it may feel like I was pinching you because of my fingernail, you may feel pressure on your knee, yes at some point you may think, *okay this is going on a little too long and it's a little weird and strange.* That would pop into your head but then I want you to go back to immediately feeling your physical feelings. You will do this for one minute a day, two minutes a day, 30 seconds here, one minute here, there. Whenever you can, allow yourself to feel that physical feeling. Whenever you have a moment, you will work on this new skill.

It's easier to do this when you are having an argument or confrontation and you're feeling those physical feelings of anxiety inside your body. But I want you to be able to just describe them without analyzing them. You're like a detective. You're sitting in observation of your physical feelings, and you are doing that several times a day as often as you possibly can. Do not attempt to make the feelings come or go, it is not about you controlling it, it is not about you making something happen. It is simply about you taking your brain, your mind, and focusing inside your body at different areas wherever you choose.

Please take notes of your physical feelings over the next week.

The Treatment

I want you to just be able to experience what that feels like and describe it. Again, you're not going into your head to analyze, you are staying inside the body and feeling what that feels like. You may have to remove yourself from others and go to a back room to feel your physical feelings. Do this one minute today, two minutes a day, one minute here, there whenever you can. Do not attempt to set a time or attempt to make something happen but you are taking your brain, your mind, and focusing inside your body. Focusing on different areas wherever you choose.

You may try what is called a body scan. The body scan starts at the top of our head and slowly, we move down through the entire body, feeling your neck, shoulders, chest, and your organs as we end at our feet, feeling the bottom of our feet. If you have time, you may reverse that process and move from the bottom of your feet to the top of your head, noticing how you are physically feeling along the way.

We are staying with this exercise for several weeks. This is the foundation of this work. When you are anxiety-free you will still need to sit with self. We will add to this exercise, but we will not leave it. This skill is very important, and you will need to work on it for weeks to come. Because it is a skill, a skill takes time to develop so there is no timeline in sitting with self.

After working on sitting with self for two weeks, please feel free to progress in the treatment.

Stage 3

Repairing Your Disconnection

Everything's Not a 10

At this stage, stage 3, we are looking at chapter 2, "Disconnection: Training, Trying, and Trauma." From now on in each stage please review and work on my sitting with self technique. If you need to review what that means, please look at the first paragraph on the top of page 40 that Patricia Evans has written. Again, be sure and keep detailed notes on your thoughts and feelings, how it currently relates to your life, and how it has related to your past and your childhood.

At the bottom of page 40, we are looking at a story that is told about a day in the life of Jack, a child, and his parents Dick and Jane. The story is basically one of how we survive in childhood, the pain of poor parenting, disconnected parenting, and invalidating parenting. That is where the disconnection originates. It works in this way; the child is in so much pain because he has a sense of self and has come here with a sense of who they are to a small degree. You do understand that you have the same heart and the same brain as you did the day that you were born. You will have the same organs the day that you die. So, it makes sense that we do come with a sense of self, a sense of who we could be. This is going to be developed by our parents through validation, through talking as a master teacher, a deliberate parent whose role is helping develop the child into adulthood. Ultimately the goal is how they see themselves. Are they confident, have they self-actualized, and do they have a sense of who they are as individuals not dependent on others and external things to define them? When that is not successful the child then has to take on the thoughts and feelings of others thereby disconnecting from their own sense of who they are as told to them by nature.

Please reflect in a very insightful way on your thoughts and feelings and how that relates to your childhood. Do you speak negatively to yourself?

The Treatment

Write examples from your life.

Moving on to page 41 we look at the third paragraph. "If we 'take in' someone else's definition of us we can believe that their own definition is more *real* than our own. We substitute our self-definition with someone else's. We come to 'know' ourselves in a backwards way from the outside in, not the inside out."

This happens of course in childhood, but you can see it more clearly in intimate relationships where the relationship is defined by how the person thinks and feels about the other person instead of what it should be. How do we support each other and be each other's biggest fans? When we are not validated in childhood by our parents, not taught that we could say no and still be loved, not taught to negotiate our own thoughts and feelings separate from our "godlike parents," we are basically taught that we will only be loved if we do and say and be all the things that our parents find important and control. We see Jack is being taught that he has to disconnect from his feelings and take on the thoughts and feelings of his parents. He must if he wants to get love from his parents, he has no choice in the matter. In childhood, how would he know any better? As we grow up, how do we learn anything different, if you go from relationship to relationship, from stage in life to stage in life and we do not have that part of the brain retrained. When corrected we are able to deny what has been taught to us in a backwards way.

These patterns continue into all of our intimate relationships. We continue them into our relationships on the playground with friends at school being bullied and bullying (one and the same), then taking

The Treatment

it into our first relationship in adolescence. That relationship has to be about control and chaos. We marry this and then we teach our children that there is no inner peace, there is only control and chaos and finding fault and moving from relationship to relationship without acceptance and inner peace.

Let us continue in the book on page 41. Look at the three italicized points. *"He would lose some sense of awareness."* This simply means that when we have anxiety, we are so disconnected that it is a disconnection of what we physically feel. This feeling can be to the human touch. You see this in some of your involvements in intimate relationships, a sexual relationship, you are not as available to feel the touch of your partner. You are not fully in the moment. Sex will change for you as you move out of disconnection. When we look at people with multiple piercings which are quite painful we ask ourselves, how do they endure that pain? Cutting and self-harm are a cry for attention. It is also driven by a want to feel something, to feel anything. As you get older you begin to disconnect and not feel pain, not feel your physical sensations. As you move out of anxiety and you become more centered you become fully centered, fully present it is then, at that time that you can feel that physical touch 100%.

"He would lose emotional awareness." If you have not learned to figure out how you feel, how would you also understand the thoughts and feelings of others? If you cannot relate, have empathy, know what pain or tears are, and experience no joy, are fully in yourself, in your own life, it will be very difficult for

you to understand it in others. This is the consequence again of that lack of validation, that lack of empathy in parenting.

"He would lose his intuitive awareness." This intuition is extremely important as we are young but also if we can remain centered and focused throughout our entire lives it can make us more able to make decisions. A decision is not about making it with our head only, it is about making it with all of our senses present, fully able to actualize the information to our senses and therefore make a proper informed decision on many more levels than just our backwards thinking. Confidence in the ability to listen to the senses is extremely important as you move through childhood and adolescence, it is what keeps us safe. It can tell you who is healthy for you and what is healthy for you. If we are able to tap into that body and mind connection, we can sense what is good for us moment to moment.

The Treatment

Describe how you lose awareness:

1. Physical sensation:

2. Emotional:

3. Intuitive:

On page 42 we have the story that I use frequently about the ice cream and how it is very common that parents tell children exactly how they think and feel by telling them what they like. In this story of course, the child is not able to withstand the emotional insults and poor boundaries from her mother. The parents are all-knowing/God-like, and so the child will take it in as truth because the child wants to, needs to, to be loved by her parents. Therefore, she will take on what they say and how they treat her as her truth. We begin to understand the concept of psychic boundaries as we look to the bottom of page 42 and understand these boundaries are about how you are treated.

Describe how your parents assaulted your psychic boundaries.

Look on page 43 in the center of the page: "Without consistent affirmation, it is easy for a child to take in a parent's definition of his or her own inner reality." As you may recall, a child's boundaries are open to receiving nurturing protection. Please keep in mind that part of why we're using this chapter is to have a vocabulary that you will use moving forward and certainly boundaries are extremely important. Again, when we learn to have boundaries, we are to figure out what is working for us best without consistent affirmation from others. That definition discusses that a parent can certainly put into a child exactly their point of view. It sounds rather obvious, but the fact of the matter is that the child doesn't know any better, but the parents will say that the child picks their personality traits up outside of the home. Learned behavior begins in the home from the parental figures. The point of view that self-worth and self-esteem are established by someone outside of the home is not true although certain things do come into play. The foundation of children's psychology is the primary responsibility of our parents.

What is your understanding of boundaries in childhood? What were you taught by your parental figures? Reflect below.

Moving to page 44, look at the bottom of the page. Since Dick and Jane intended to be good parents what could rest them from their empathy for their own child? Understand that intentions in life are meaningless. If we intend to pay our rent/mortgage or go to work but do not, we get nowhere and achieve nothing. So, parenting has to be looked at in the same manner. We should be able to look at our child and see the challenges they are experiencing. When we cannot, as Dick and Jane could not, did not, it was a lack of empathy. How could they learn empathy if they never received empathy from their parents? And so the legacy of abuse and neglect continues. We can't teach something that we never had, unless we acknowledge it and work to change.

Part of the process of sitting with self is to learn and teach ourselves how to be empathetic. How we do that is by going into our body as we are feeling our physical feelings and when we pop into our head with a negative thought (because when we have anxiety, most of our thoughts are negative, whether we realize it or not) we do not judge, become frustrated or upset nor do we allow it to grow, we don't live there anymore. We now move back into the body. So that back-and-forth process of going into the body and into the head continues over and over again. Each time you are in your head, simply and quietly move it back into the body. From moment to moment we are feeling our feelings, quietly and peacefully.

Do you understand that your current choices are based on your parents' past choices for you?

Write examples below.

Describe and recall how your parents defined you.

The Treatment

We are moving forward as we begin to understand that there are three types of anxiety. As we feel those physical feelings in our body three things are occurring. By now you have also made a list of those physical feelings. You may have five or 25. These physical feelings are extremely important because they are unique to you. Every time we feel one of those physical feelings we are going to place our minds inside our body if only for 30 seconds. We are then going to call it out as I call it

There are three types of anxiety: 1) You are having distorted thinking, your thought process is wrong. 2) You are someplace you are not supposed to be. 3) Someone in front of you is trying to control you. That someone might be in your phone, your computer or a real person in front of your face.

When we feel our physical feelings and call it out, we are not overthinking. We have to acknowledge that we know our thinking is backwards, so we can no longer rely solely on our thoughts. We are using our bodies from now on. Again, our thinking is backwards, and we are simply acknowledging it and going back into the body with that information.

So again, why you are having the physical feelings that you are having are of three choices: 1) You are having negative thinking. Your thought process is wrong, it's distorted thinking (refer to page 17 when Evans writes "a distortion or lack of awareness"). 2) You are someplace you are not supposed to be. You are surrounded by negativity, by a person, a situation, there is something that your body is telling you, that this is not healthy for you. This could be a negative place or prior to some negative event that is brewing around you. 3) You're being controlled by someone or something (such as your phone or computer). As we move through this process, we will learn what to do with each of them in each situation.

Stage 4

Three Types of Anxiety

Interpreting Your Feelings Correctly

Again, we are reviewing the sitting with self technique. You are simply allowing yourself to feel your physical feelings. You understand that you will move in and out of your body and into your negative thinking and that is perfectly ok. Each time you understand your negative thinking is like a trap door that is slowly closing on the right side of your brain, eventually it will fall away, and you will shift yourself to your positive thinking (the left side of your brain) naturally. Understand that this negative thinking is unhealthy—it's dark and it is what has held you back, it has never served you and it never will.

We will move in and out of that process a thousand times if we need to as the negativity slowly drops away. When we find our center and feel our physical feelings we then move in and out as we learn how to call it out. We understand that we are having distorted thinking and negative thought processes and we are now shifting that and retraining the brain to have positive thoughts.

Again, there are three types of anxiety.

1) We are having distorted thinking; our thought process is wrong. We do not need to analyze this, we just trust our body's physical feeling

and shift our thought to a positive thought of what is my truth.

Example: I am not injured or in danger, the love I have for myself is what is real, I am present in what I am doing at this moment (more on that later).

2) We are some place we are not supposed to be. We will remove ourselves quickly from a situation to protect ourselves to save ourselves or we will get a plan to do so.

3) Someone in front of you is trying to control you. With this type of anxiety, we will move away from electronics, anything or anyone trying to control us. We will block, delete or turn off. We will set boundaries with an individual who stands in front of us by using words such as "this is not working for me," "please don't talk to me like that," and "you have a right to your opinion, and I have an inherent right to mine." We must now learn to always do what is best for us. To listen to our bodies.

In this instance, boundaries are not taught in childhood as the child has no voice, no one asks and respects the anxious child's thoughts or feelings. A parent with an anxious child said, "I asked her why she was crying, and she didn't know and that was why I ignored her." Good parenting is not about getting answers, but asking questions and not having a need to control the outcome. If an answer is given, great. If not, great. The goals are to teach how to think and feel as an individual. This thinking in an individual creates confidence and a healthy self-esteem.

Take time to write your notes about your boundaries and when you gave yourself a voice.

Let's move on to page 45.

"Distortion occurs whenever one person defines another person." Here Evans is basically helping you to understand that no one can tell you how you think, and you cannot tell others how they think and feel. From this point on when someone tells us how they think and feel we are going to take it on as an absolute truth if they say it, then it must be true. We have to begin to learn how we think and feel and understand that other people have the same capability. This speaks to number three; the type of anxiety that says someone in front of you is trying to control you. We will be responsible for all of our thoughts and feelings and we will also embrace them and learn the technique of centering ourselves enough to know exactly how we think and feel, and the confidence to verbalize how we think and feel. We are no longer listening to those voices from our childhood that define us and tell us that we have to be in control of how other people think about us.

Looking further on page 45, "Because we have not understood psychic boundaries, indeed, have only very recently begun to understand the psyche." This speaks to the type of anxiety that says I have to control how you think and feel about me so that you can love and accept me. The child learned this from the parent who constantly said you are never good enough by verbalizing negativity to the child about all of their decisions, thoughts and feelings. People with anxiety are very good at learning to be what others want them to be. So, this is a life of surrounding yourself with people who do not know or care for you.

The Treatment

As we sit with self the negative thinking drops away and we see that when we allow negative people in our lives, they stand in the way of the positive people who will love and accept you for whomever you choose to be. All negativity is a lie, so we allow it to drop away because it never served us and never will.

As we sit with self, we understand that when we are disconnected from our own thoughts and feelings it is very challenging to understand the feelings of others.

On page 46, we are looking at the word empathy and understanding the importance of learning empathy for ourselves. First understanding that we are not perfect, we do not need to be perfect and, in fact, we're looking for people who accept us for exactly who we are. We can no longer be in the business of attempting to control how other people think and feel about us.

The truth of the matter is that if you need to make someone love you, in fact, they do not love you, they love the idea of you. We can only look for the positive people who see us exactly for who we are. We have got to get to the full understanding that living for and taking on the thoughts and feelings of others is shortening our lives.

Are you empathetic?

Give examples of both being empathic and empathetic.

The Treatment

What are some of your distortions?

Anxiety: Curing the New Normal

Look at the bottom of page 46. The story of the little boy who was raised in a backwards way is obvious abuse, but it was not obvious to him. Evans writes "How could I have known anything different?" His view of his childhood was normal, and he also normalized his disconnected emotions. I have never had a patient who didn't tell me that they had a great childhood. Most blame themselves for being abused and neglected. With that point of view, how can we raise sane children when they are ultimately responsible for raising themselves?

There are some stories currently in the news and in the media in which children in their 20s are abusing their peers some to the point of suicide, simply because this is how they were taught: that relationships look like abuse, neglect and control or there is no relationship. It is the parents who should be held responsible, because of the lack of empathy that both young adults have is the lack of empathy in parenting and ultimately the result of depression and anxiety.

Page 47 is the final page we will reference in this chapter, with the heading "Trying to Disconnect." It is very significant when we talk about wanting to be disconnected, getting used to it as we get older, normalizing our pain, normalizing our dysfunctional relationships, and normalizing our lack of inner peace. We are moving away from that for good. We are understanding that in this description the only way to survive is to try and disconnect, we had to try and survive, but you have survived. The last paragraph on page 47 talks about the gentleman who loses his temper. It is about the need to control. Understanding that it is not so easy, just to wish these thoughts and feelings away from our childhood is not possible. We have to dig them out like the cancer that they are, this negativity learned in childhood again has been normalized and we are now in a place to see clearly and understand it. Evans writes "the only feeling he seemed able to identify was anger." We have not been able to stop the anger and negative behaviors until now. We have been angry at our fears, angry at ourselves. We can now let go of that old voice and idea that has kept us small.

Stage 5

Depression

The Depression Train

Although there is quite a bit of information available to us about depression, we are still not able to understand what it looks like and its various stages, and the nuances of how it affects our daily living. Depression is like cancer; it has several stages. There is no anxiety without depression. Depression is the wood to the fire of anxiety. Once the fire is out only more wood will rekindle the fire.

Living with depression at any stage is problematic, sometimes impossible, and eventually, it progresses to a stage in which life is chaotic but somehow normalized and excused in society. When I first started my practice and began understanding depression, I was like most thinking that depression was sadness, it was something that a human body can control through thought. I was against medication and saw that in some way medication was a crutch. I have progressed due to my need to become a depression expert. Out of my ability to cure anxiety, I learned that there is no curing anxiety without treating and stabilizing depression. Depression is a chemical imbalance and there are many reasons why and how that chemical imbalance is present, but it should be fully understood that living with that imbalance is a life drain at any stage. This drain is totally unnecessary and the longer that you put off treatment of your depression the longer you are delayed in fully living and the more progressive your depression will become.

Why wait until you move out of stage one of depression? If you received treatment earlier, you could have done so many things in your youth. Once you have your depression stabilized, being stable would probably prevent you from moving into those other stages or slow the process down greatly.

As an example, I had a patient who was a master's level psychology student on the verge of graduating yet when I told him he had depression he became very irate and angry at me for imparting my diagnosis of him. I stated to him that we can discuss it another time, but we do have to discuss it at some point. He continued to come to therapy, and we treated his anxiety. One day he arrived stating that he understood depression. He stated to me that he thought about it and while he was on the New York City subway taking the A train (a subway train that travels a huge distance to many boroughs here in New York City) he realized that depression is like a train; it has many stops. "You can get off at the first stop or you can stay on but eventually you will go to the end and you will get off." I asked him if I, with the help of my interns, could put this into a diagram that explains this in detail and what some and only some of the traits of those many stages of depression look like in a life. Please see the following illustration.

The Treatment

Stops on the Depression Train

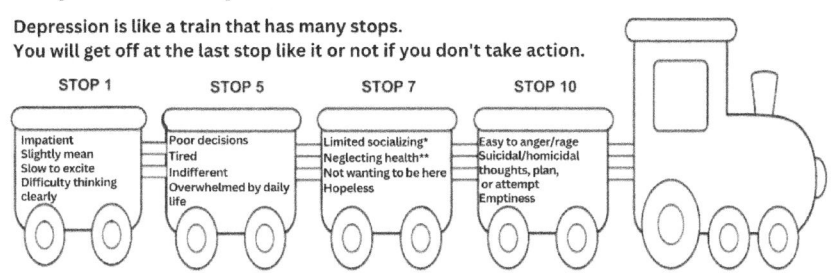

Depression is like a train that has many stops.
You will get off at the last stop like it or not if you don't take action.

STOP 1	STOP 5	STOP 7	STOP 10
Impatient Slightly mean Slow to excite Difficulty thinking clearly	Poor decisions Tired Indifferent Overwhelmed by daily life	Limited socializing* Neglecting health** Not wanting to be here Hopeless	Easy to anger/rage Suicidal/homicidal thoughts, plan, or attempt Emptiness

Key words:
*Limited socializing: Regular outings with friends or partner, NOT including family.
** Neglected health: Not cleaning body. Not going to dentist or medical providers regularly.

The statistics are that 70% of the American population has mental illness. At this time during the pandemic's end it is even higher. It has long been thought in my profession that only a small number of individuals have severe mental illness (schizophrenia, any personality disorder) which can at best be managed. If that is the case, then the majority of the dysfunction is depression and anxiety. You can have depression without anxiety but when there is anxiety there is always depression.

It always amazes me that people who have depression or don't know they have depression, attribute their depression to the chaos and misfortune and then unhappiness in their lives as just life itself. Another thing that I find baffling in those suffering with depression is that even if they acknowledge that they have depression they react as if it is normal and as if it has no bearing on their daily lives.

When someone is told they have depression, the other common reaction is anger (which by itself is a major trait of depression). My profession also minimizes depression and does not have the courage, strength, or interest to study depression even though it is thought to be the number one mental illness in the United States. Perhaps we minimize it because we are struggling and unable to stabilize ourselves. How can I stabilize a patient if I can't get there myself?

Understanding and treating depression is not difficult, but we need a 21st century way of looking at depression. It should be fully understood that living with depression and a lack of balance is a lifetime struggle yet unnecessary. The longer that you put off treatment of it the longer you are delaying living fully. My older patients cry when they stabilize. They cry for wasting their lives and the anger they experience that no one around them helped them in a lifetime.

We move on and get to the business of having a joyful life. Why wait until you worsen and move out of stop 1 with depression when you could have done so much more living once you have your depression stabilized. It always amazes me that people who have depression or don't know they have depression view the depression and chaos and then happiness as misfortune and just life itself. Another thing that I find daunting is that they have the viewpoint that there is nothing they can do about it and again just one more thing they have to live with.

Treating Depression

I have a system that is painstaking and must be followed exactly, but after years of trial and error I have found what works. If you are on ANY medications you must discuss these options with your provider. Most providers (primary care physicians and specialists who are not necessarily psychopharmacologists) have a great knowledge of nutraceuticals, so ask them before you try my suggestions. The other four points of a five-point self-care plan are about leaning into nature. Doing what you MUST do to be here on the planet. If you want an A+ life then you will need to get an A+ on your self-care plan.

1. **Nutraceuticals/Vitamins.** If you are under 24 (the age in which the brain is done developing) you might begin your journey using all-natural anti-depressants. St. John's wort, SAM-e, 5HTP. Do your best to find a psychopharmacologist who works with nutraceuticals and natural remedies.

If you are over 25 you may need to look at synthetic antidepressants over anti-anxiety medication. Anti-anxiety drugs always have an addictive component and because we are curing anxiety naturally we may not need that type of drug. Not only that, they do not stop anxiety. They certainly may reduce some symptoms but because it is easily cured, taking anxiety drugs could be creating a more challenging addiction problem. If you have ever taken anxiety drugs, the fact that anxiety can eat through any drug and leave you with symptoms should teach you the power of the mind. That being said, in the current condition of our planet, an anti-anxiety drug can keep you from an 8-9 or 10 on our depression scale which can save a life and help you help yourself. Take it. It can be a bridge so that you can work on leaving your anxiety behind you.

No matter what you hear, the timing of when you take your antidepressant can make or break the effects. Most antidepressants should be taken midmorning between 9-11:30am. I know this because of the extensive questions I ask my patients to get to the bottom of how the medication works for them and that you must understand that just taking a pill will NOT work. This point is exacting. I have a patient who takes her medication to the minute and when she doesn't, she feels awful. The later she takes the medication the longer her instability lasts.

The timing has to do with how long the medication is in and out of the body and the body's sensitivity to blood changes, especially for women.

If it is your goal to take your nutraceuticals and not ever think about it then you will need to adhere to my suggestions each day. Look at it like brushing your teeth. You don't forget, nor do you complain. (If you DO, you have depression, unless you're 4 years old). Antidepressants take up to 6-12 months to see the full effects. You should take a starter dose and increase to a normal dose. This is called the slow and low method. You take a small dose and allow yourself to feel how it makes you feel and if you have any effects. We can better add our vitamins and nutraceuticals with this slow and low method. We wait for several days to add our vitamins and several weeks to increase the medication dose if needed. You will be on the starter dose for one month or longer before you get to your regular dose. Antidepressant effects are like dust, you do feel them but it's a little bit each and every day. There are milestones of the first 30 days and then 90 days and then six months and a year. My patients are always amazed that they still feel the increase in insight and clarity even after a year. Please talk to your medical provider about all of your plans and goals. You have got to be honest and find someone that you can hear and they can hear you. DO YOUR RESEARCH.

2. Sleep is not an option. Sleeping seven to nine hours each and every night is imperative. Most people who have anxiety have poor sleep hygiene. They sleep too much or too little. I suggest tart cherry (pill form 1000mg) taken in the evening (this is not for everyone, there are some contraindications with some medications). This makes melatonin in your system, so the sleep is natural, and you do not have to take this each night. You should take it for one week and then gauge how you are doing. I check in each night with my patients because the truth is that sleep is at least 50% of your issues when you have depression. This is my secret weapon. It's discouraging when my profession doesn't realize this.

The first day of my educational internship at Fordham University my teacher, after hearing my diagnosis for a group of 25 toddlers, asked me if I had asked them about their sleep. I said, "No, what does sleep have to do with anything?" Once I researched the importance of sleep in children I understood. I took my knowledge back to the parents of my 25 "clients" and after only one-week half of the "clients" dropped out citing they were better. Sleeping seven to nine hours each night is not optional.

3. Exercise and Sun. Get sunlight in your face each day and I am not talking about suntanning. Have your vitamin D levels checked by your primary care physician. Most people who have depression have low vitamin D levels. You can get vitamin D through sunlight. In the winter months, you can take it in synthetic pill form. Too much vitamin D can be toxic, so it is not advised to take each day for an extended period of time. Alternate with sitting in the sun when you are able. It is not a mystery that when my depressed patient goes to a sunny vacation destination they report low to no depression.

Make every attempt to combine that sun exposure with exercise each and every day. Not every therapist should say this, but there is a way to get that exercise each day. If you want to keep your depression very low without medication (or minimal meds), then exercising at an athletic level must be done. Short of intense exercising you can walk for 10 minutes each day (no matter the temperature). If you look for small ways to get outside, you can build slowly. Also, when you feel better it's easier to do more.

Exercise, like so many things, can have so many rules attached to it. Learn to let go of the rules and have fun being in nature. Perhaps that means joining a walking club or it becomes what you do with your partner or children. If we look at exercise only to lose weight, we are missing out on enjoying life. Expand your understanding of exercise and make it part of how you socialize.

4. Eating good food. I am not talking about a diet to lose weight. I'm talking about watching your sugar and alcohol intake. Watching it means noticing the effects it has on your body when you ingest it. This can help you learn to regulate sugar and alcohol. This is low on my list only because when you have depression eating properly is just not going to happen. You

The Treatment

don't have the clear thinking to address it or have it not appear overwhelming. Again, the more your depression decreases the more you are able to see all things much clearer. More than one or two alcoholic drinks is deadly to your mood and worse if you are taking anti-depressants.

The mix of alcohol and antidepressants can be life-threatening. Alcohol is a depressant, so you will NEVER see the full effects of your anti-depressant even if you drink periodically. It's best to wait the year into taking your anti-depressant and then discuss drinking alcohol with your medical provider. No matter what, more than a few drinks a week will prevent you from stabilizing your depression. As we age we have to be prepared to let go of processed food. Look to eat as clean a diet as you can. See a nutritionist. Read and try new things. Eliminate all boxed and prepared food.

5. Socialization. At your low level of depression, you wait for an invitation to socialize. This comes fairly easily when you are young but as you get older if you don't keep up your interpersonal relationships outside of your family you will be isolated in your later years. During the mid-stage of depression, you feel like you are socializing because you are with your family. You allow your elderly parents or your children to be the excuse that you don't have a life. Socialization means that you have a set of activities that you do just for you with your chosen peer group. This should be what you look forward to and on a weekly (if not more) basis at a minimum. Again, this is not about having dozens of friends but perhaps a shared experience group and then two to three close friends.

It cannot be overstated that it is imperative to find a medical provider who understands holistic medicine. This was unheard of just 10 years ago and now the opposite is true. Most medical professionals have some knowledge of nutraceuticals and even specialize in a holistic practice. My list is a guide for your research and further discussion with your doctor. If a doctor says I don't know anything about holistic medicine then you asking them their opinion is futile.

The results of my technique have been unique and patients who have suffered for years report minimal to no anxiety within a year of the treatment. I have a system of checking to see the level of clarity of thought and the habits that they are building are an indication that they have no anxiety and understand how to stabilize their depression.

We are learning the life lesson first and foremost about what is healthy for us and therefore we call ourselves to the positive people in our lives. We actively call positive people to us. We are retraining our brain to remain in the positive so that we deflect and deny negative thinking and gravitate and attract the positive. We are learning to let go of all negativities that we currently attract. We don't listen or define our relationships by labels; "mother," "father," "sister" or "partner." If you are attempting to control me then I must survive and take care of myself by setting boundaries. "You are not me and you don't know how I feel unless you ask me." Further, you will figure out how you feel by turning to nature to guide you. You will lean toward your own thoughts and feelings and have confidence that you will understand your likes and dislikes and you will prevail.

In the next section please take careful and deliberate notes.

Stage 6

Positive Thinking

Leaning into the Sun

In stage six, we are acknowledging old behavior and retraining the brain.

It's best to start out by telling you what positive thinking is not.

1. It's not that you see the glass half full. In order for you to see the glass as half full you would have to notice the negative in the glass in the first place. Negative thinking is you learning from your parental figures that something is missing or needs improvement. No one put you in charge of pointing out what is needed in most areas. We are consultants with the goal to inspire in all that we do in life, especially with our children and our partner.

2. If you feel or think that whenever you get this done or that accomplished, or when that happens then I will be happy, you are thinking negatively. The here and now is perfect. If there is no imminent danger or pain, there is joy.

3. Focusing on the future is not appreciating the current moment. This is negative thinking. The beauty of life is in the details of this moment.

My Definition of Positive Thinking:
The ability to see and feel kindness, beauty, and joy, then to acknowledge it right here, in this and each moment of each day, every day, all day.

We are not Pollyannas, secure in fantasy. If we see or feel wrong or hurt, we acknowledge it, if we are able to take up cause (and we must) let us do so with focus and a pure heart with all of our senses present and with passion.

Let's interpret that definition:
The ability to see and feel kindness, beauty and joy then acknowledge it. This means that we are able to be fully present moment to moment, that there is always some joy going on in every moment of our lives, and we are able to see it. We are able to acknowledge it right there at that moment every day, all day. When we choose, we can see beauty and joy if we allow ourselves. We must practice and focus each moment of every day seeing what makes us happy—from a cup of coffee, to a smile, to a flower or the smell of the air.

We are not Pollyannas, secure in fantasy. Pollyanna was an old book about a woman who only saw everything as perfect, no matter how bad it was. This is not us. We see things for what they really are.

When we see or feel something we acknowledge it.
This doesn't mean we strike out in anger. It means we are entitled to all of our feelings, just not our behavior.

If we are able to take a cause. This means that we each must find the activist in us. We might focus our efforts on our own family or our community. How can we best serve? Our anxiety makes us complain and not take action but we can live our best lives and be a role model or we can actively do something in our lives to help take care of other people doing this with a pure heart without anxiety. You are not doing it so that you could become famous or rich or because your mother wanted you to do this. You're taking up a cause because you have passion for it, you are fully present in your life, you show up to be the best that you can be at what you have passion for in your life each and every day.

Each day we are moving out of our brainwashing from childhood. We are resetting our original state of feelings of confidence. Nature gave us that because it is here for us. It is our guide. Confidence is what we are selling in all that we do. Tell yourself "I can do anything because I can figure it out by taking MY time, listening to myself, and doing what I think and feel." If it doesn't work out for me then it was not meant for me and I learned more about myself so that is why I can trust my confidence.

Positive thinking requires we make a decision each day not to judge what others want to do, but focus on the joy of our lives and let the lies of negative thinking fall away naturally because it never served us, and it never will.

All negative thinking is a lie. Think about it. No one is out to harm you; they just might not have your best interest at heart, or they are wounded and that cannot be your journey. Wish them well and move on with the business of your journey. That is your job: to know yourself, your soul, your voice. I am not suggesting that you not help others, but help yourself first and then use your strength to help those that WANT to be helped. The highest form of helping is not giving of things but usually a positive word or more importantly a positive thought about a person. That is powerful beyond belief.

We don't fully understand that concept because our parental figures did not tell us that we were just incredible people and meant it in the deepest part of their hearts. We can choose to do things differently. We must understand that if you have a negative situation and you add negativity to it then you WILL get a negative outcome. Stop thinking that a negative plus a negative will give you a positive. If you have a negative approach to your children, partner, or work then don't be shocked or upset that it doesn't give you the fantasy positive outcome. Let's leave that childish immature thinking in our past once and for all.

At this time, we are continuing to learn the sitting with self technique by practicing it every single day for 30 seconds here, one minute here, two minutes here, each and every day as often as we possibly can. The goal is to heal and center the self. The healing is by hearing and validating your own feelings. Remember, we are just talking about physical feelings and then we add on. We are going into the body and feeling our physical feelings. We are calling out the three types of anxiety once we identify those physical feelings and doing what we described.

The sitting with self technique is the foundation to this work. It is the cornerstone to retraining the brain. It is what nature wants us to do, to go inside the body and feel our physical feelings. We are not analyzing, not going into the head to think. If we go into the head and we have a negative thought and it begins to grow, we quickly move it back into the body. What we don't do is judge it or question how or why we have to have a negative thought about going into the head. We can do this a thousand times a day, each time shifting into the body naturally with empathy.

It is with this process that we teach ourselves empathy. Empathy starts at home. We do not go into our heads and judge ourselves and talk negatively about ourselves. We go into the body like a detective, and we are simply holding on different parts in the body. This may take on a meditative state yet that is not what we are doing because we are conscious, conscious and present in our own bodies.

We can do what is called a body scan which is to start at the top of the head and feel our physical feelings all the way through our body, through our neck, our shoulders, our lungs and our breathing. Also, feeling our heart, moving towards our stomach or intestinal areas, to our pelvic area down to our legs, knees and through our legs, to the bottom of our feet, to the tips of our toes. We can then reverse this process or stop at any time and pick up at any time.

This sitting with self technique is one we will hold onto through this entire process. If at any time when you check in with yourself you will ask yourself *am I sitting with self? Is that part of my life and my self-care plan?* It is certainly easy to feel your physical feelings in an altercation or a confrontation whether you are confronting someone or someone is confronting you. We feel those physical feelings of anxiety in our body so we can remove ourselves if need be. We can go into another room (going into the bathroom or the kitchen) and take 30 seconds because this is an exercise for now that will turn into a way of life. And so, through this time of exercising sitting with self we want to be able to physically remove ourselves (walk away) and consciously feel our physical feelings. As we move through this we will do it more and more but the process of sitting with self for 30 seconds, one minute, just having a time in which you sit with self, perhaps in the shower, when you wake up, before you get out of bed, before you fall asleep; that is how you can make this a conscious decision to go into the body. You must practice your physical feelings often.

It is now that you will have a clarity of thinking and the acute ability to see the dysfunction of others and reflect that dysfunction in your own life. You are now just moving through life seeing how others are thinking backwards and moving in a backwards way.

Please reflect on your positive thinking and what you see in your day to day life. Where do you now see the joy?

Stage 7

Boundaries Are Everything

"Pretending and Its Impact" is the final chapter in *Controlling People* we will reflect upon in this book. Most people tell me that at this stage they find this one gives them complete clarity and makes the most sense to them. Further, it provides them with an understanding of where they have come from. As we shift our thinking we can now give ourselves permission to change some behaviors that no longer work for us.

When we look at page 58 Patricia Evans writes, "When people 'make up' your reality–as if they were you–they are trying to control you even when they don't realize it." We are talking about something that has been normalized and continues to be normalized in our everyday life, in our interpersonal relationships, and expressly in our parenting. Each and every day you make a decision whether to listen to your own body, what is going on inside of you or what is outside of you, what is external, how things and people define you, what your childhood was, who says what to you, what you believe based on how other people think and feel. In this process, you are learning that going inside of your body and allowing that to guide you and to lead you is what will now work for you.

Moving down page 58 to the fourth paragraph. "We know that they are pretending because in actual fact no one can tell you what you want to believe in, do or why you have done what you have done." This is a very positive, powerful statement because it helps us really see in black and white that what she says is so correct and so meaningful. You are your own person and from moment to moment and no matter what the relationship is, we cannot be defined by definitions, not even by labels of relationships.

Those labels of mother, father, partner, child or friend are meaningless when it comes to knowing yourself, feeling what you feel, getting in touch and having a voice of your own. It doesn't mean that we can't take in other people's information, it just means that it will never override our thoughts and our own feelings and what is best for us.

The final paragraph on 58 states, "Despite the evidence, it is difficult for many people to realize that the person who defines them is not being rational. They feel inclined to defend themselves as if the person defending them is rational. But by trying to defend them against someone's definition, they are acknowledging those definitions as valid, that they make sense, when they are in fact complete nonsense."

We can interpret that simply: if you validate nonsense by discussing it, by attempting to make a person understand that they are talking nonsense, then you are giving it power. You are also that hamster on a wheel. That hamster on a wheel goes round and round and round and at any time we can make a decision to get off, but once we are on again, we cannot complain about where it goes, what happened, or what is happening to us. There are consequences in disconnection from self when we get on that wheel.

The Treatment

We are entitled to all of our thoughts and all of our feelings every single day, all day.

Moving on to page 60, we look at the top paragraph that talks about how the backwards thinking of our leaders has been normalized. This continues in our everyday life in all of our personal relationships. If we hire a train conductor and ask him to conduct surgery, then it is our backwards thinking, not theirs. We need to look at our willingness to ask something of someone who is not suited. Negative thinking grows so once you begin that process it builds momentum and you are now pulling that negative backwards thinking to you in all that you do.

On the middle of page 60, we look at the italicized paragraph: *"What blinds people the most to controlling behavior is the belief that the person who consistently defines them truly loves them."* Again, that is reinforcing backwards thinking. The backwards idea that a love relationship looks controlling, that it looks like you must know me, you know me more than I know myself. *I am dependent on you to know me more* is backwards thinking taught to the child by the parental figure.

Evans gives this example, "One of the saddest cases I have encountered was that of a woman who believed her mate loved her so much only he could tell her the *real* truth about herself. Although she was highly intelligent (as tests later proved) and an extraordinarily gifted singer (as early evaluations noted), she thought that she was 'not smart' and had an 'unremarkable' voice."

You could want to think that he is responsible for making her feel less than, but the fact of the matter is that when we raise a child with positive thinking and self-esteem they would not be phased by invalidation because they would not allow it in their personal lives. We do that by validating our children's thoughts and their feelings, by helping them feel their feelings. We must cultivate their thinking by asking them questions and not consistently and continuously telling them how to think, what to do, and asking, "Are you sure?" The mere act of allowing our children to make simple decisions and then decisions that shape their lives builds their self-esteem. From decisions about what they want to eat, what they want to wear, to how they want to conduct their day. These behaviors and thought patterns build their self-esteem. That self-esteem will be reflected in their choices throughout their life.

On the surface, it could look as though the partner is responsible for making her feel less than, but the fact of the matter is that when we raise a child with positive thinking and with self-esteem then we do not allow negativity and invalidation into our lives. We do that by validating our children's thoughts and then feelings.

This thinking and behavior are reinforcing what are ideas from childhood of a love relationship that is controlling. The belief becomes, "You must control me to love me and love me to control me." Further, "You must know me, and you also know me more than I know myself." "I am dependent on you to know me." All of these beliefs are examples of backwards thinking.

On the bottom of page 60 in the last paragraph, Evans writes, "Inner certainty is hard to come by if one's own truth, one's own very being, is constantly

The Treatment

denied." This objectification of a person, the fact that they are a child, our child, does not give up permission not to treat them as a whole person with human feelings. If I am constantly telling or asking a child, "Are you sure you don't want that, you don't need that, are you positive that you want that, why would you choose that?" you are adding doubt. By constantly questioning a child's thinking they are going to feel as though they cannot think. They will believe they don't have a right to think and that muscle from childhood will build, making them believe it is normal for others to think for them. The child concludes they don't have a right to think, and they need others to think for them.

Moving on to page 61, in the third paragraph, Evans writes, "As we lose self-awareness, we lose our ability to respond to our inner needs. We may not even know what they are; 'I guess I do like chocolate-walnut best.'" Therein lies the depression that is created when we are not allowed to have our own thoughts and feelings. Depression starts in very early childhood and lingers into our adulthood and into our intimate relationships and in every piece of our lives.

Further, Evans writes, "Every time we accept someone else's definition of our own inner reality, we set aside our own experience and so lose awareness." Think about what that means to you in your interpersonal relationships. How do we set aside time to develop our thoughts and feelings if it has not been done in childhood? These are the questions that we want to deeply reflect during this stage. Reflect on how you have moved from your natural instincts of listening to yourself and realize all along, that's what was keeping you safe and present. We can move back to that at any time. We have that presence of mind with us always and we always have.

She writes at the top of 62, "An all-too-common outcome of lost self-trust is that of having extreme difficulty in making choices: 'I don't know what I *should* do.'" When we raise a child with positive thinking and with self-esteem then we do not allow negativity and invalidation into our lives. We do that by validating our children's thoughts and then feelings thereby helping them identify their feelings. The deliberate parent teaches them how to think by asking them questions and not requiring an answer. The parent who consistently tells them how to think and what to do and asks the child if they are sure creates an adult who can't make a decision, looks to others over self, and never has inner peace. The mere act of allowing children to make simple decisions then allows decisions that shape their lives and builds self-esteem. Decisions about what they want to eat, what they want to wear, and how they want to conduct their life build their self-worth and positive thinking.

How would a person know what to do if they are constantly told how to think? When a parent is coming from a place of inner peace they don't feel the need to make the decision for the child, they understand the goal is to teach them how to think, not think for them. This requires patience and after all you have every single day in your child's life for at least 15 years. It is like sitting with self, it is dust and after years of Zen-like patience turns into a mountain. We now understand that our parenting doesn't lie in that

The Treatment

moment of that decision, it lies in the big picture of the long-term goal not today nor the month or the year but the child's life.

How do we teach a child to feel good about the decisions? We allow them to make decisions and see that perhaps every decision does not work out but that is not the goal, it's simply to make the decision and feel good about it. We want them to know that if it does not work out, they can always make a new decision with confidence and know that the goal is to make the decision that is right for them.

The more decisions we make the more we know ourselves and the more we know how to make more decisions. Choose to change your experiences and welcome a new creative light of ideas and call those ideas to you along with other positive people and insights. You are no longer afraid of those voices from your childhood. They don't have any power over you. You had to survive to get to where you are and you did and now you cannot just survive, you must thrive. A lot is at stake. You are replacing the old negative voices with your own voice and your own self-actualization. You understand those voices were holding you back and keeping you from your absolute truth.

Finishing page 62 Evans writes, "What happens when people are assaulted over years and end up with little or no awareness of their inner worlds." We have been pretending that we are someone others want us to be. Negativity and chaos feels natural, we are used to pain, we even find comfort in what we are used to. Today we are dropping all that holds us back. Letting go of things, people, ideas that no longer serve us or make sense.

At this time, we continue working on positive thinking and sitting with self. If you recall, those are the cornerstones of this work. The sitting with self technique is the foundation that holds the walls and then the structure. The foundation is always connecting with our physical feelings first. This is also revealing and that is healing. Revealing in that I see things clearly now. I see my role and my negative thinking; I am honest about my choices about how I choose to see all things. That clarity with being centered is being able to sit quietly inside the body in a very private way for 30 seconds or one minute or 10 minutes each and every day as many times as possible. Understanding that the more that we do that, the more that nature helps us understand that that is how we are to be functioning and existing.

When information is coming towards us again we are calling it out: 1) I'm having negative thinking, my thought process is wrong, 2) I am someplace I'm not supposed to be, or 3) Someone or something in front of me is trying to control me. If we are having negative thinking or we are unfocused, we shift into our body, acknowledging it, and moving into a positive side. If we are someplace we are not supposed to be, that certainly can include that we are in the presence of someone that is being negative, talking harshly about others, saying things that are infringing on our emotional boundaries, or simply we are in danger and our instinct is telling us, so we can remove ourselves. If we cannot remove ourselves immediately, we will get a plan to do so. If we are on social media

The Treatment

and someone is saying something that is disturbing our inner peace, we are allowed to remove ourselves permanently or temporarily. We are also allowed our boundaries which does not mean we get on the wheel (making comments or defending ourselves which gives away our power and our energy) but simply means that we can say "This is not working for me," "Please do not talk to me like that," or "This is my choice, you have your choice and I have mine and I am asking you to respect that. If you cannot respect that, that it is also perfectly fine. I can walk away from you in the relationship and find someone that does respect my truth, my process."

Ultimately when you do not walk away you are not allowing the people who would really respect you, adore you, and find you interesting, find you. It is about you because the negative people and energy that you have surrounded yourself with is getting in the way of you finding them and them finding you. When we set a boundary, we understand that we are looking for the positive in others, we are finding positive people, ideas, artistic outlets, creativity, this is what lies in confidence. The opposite of that is negative, which is dark, it is heavy, it's a lie and it always takes you down. It is never anything that you needed, and you never will, it is always a lie.

Negative thinking is always a lie. Remember that the mind grows, thoughts grow and that means it can quickly move from a 0 to a 10 if we allow it. This is not so when we consciously retrain the brain to hold positive thinking. We must be mindful that negative thinking is shortening our lives. It is creating a breeding ground for disease. Here lies the real problem with having anxiety. It is not a small minor mental infection, it is actually a huge dangerous unnecessary mental illness. When a person thinks negatively and yet expects a positive outcome this is backwards behavior/thinking and results in a lack of inner peace and success. Whether the goal was to raise your children, lead your workers, or engage your partner, negative thoughts and feelings will always lead to more negative thoughts, feelings, and outcomes.

Remember a negative thought can grow like a positive thought so when we consciously retrain the brain to hold positive thinking we must be mindful that any negativity can affect how we feel about ourselves and our lives at this time. We have poured the new cement and laid the new foundation of brick of our own voice, but it takes time to dry. We are diligent about not letting in negative ideas from people, news, music, books, or all sources. In a year's time we will be able to withstand a great deal (if we must), but today we are careful about our minds and bodies. We focus on the positive which is light and creative. We call all positive things to us, we insist, and we don't focus on any negativity as it drops away naturally. We are focused only on the positive. If something is a real problem in front of us, in our faces, we deal with that. We are no longer following or entertaining anyone or things that are attracted to negativity.

When we don't have anxiety and there is an issue, we get a plan to deal with it by taking our time and our space (sitting with self to reflect). We then move forward with the plan and let go of the stress and negative thinking that surrounds the issue. No longer do we get on the wheel with others or ourselves.

The Treatment

We are not **reacting**, we are **reflecting**. We all have bad days but the reflection will make those bad days without chaos, without the heavy negativity and altercations with people around us. Sitting with self will become part of you because the truth is that it was never far from you. You were brainwashed into thinking that you had to answer to all things external and that your internal (that which is nature, your soul) was not your truth. Your truth lies in how you think, how you feel, what works for you in each and every moment of each and every day.

Please write how you changed a reaction into a reflection.

Stage 8

Living an Elevated Life

Stage 8 is the continued effort to elevate your positive thinking.

How do we surround ourselves with positive creative people that inspire us with encouragement and support? We seek these individuals out and don't settle for anyone else. We find our elevated thinking in podcasts, videos, readings, writing, and any media source that lifts us and assists us in maintaining our positive life and influence of our inner and outer circle of loved ones.

Living an elevated life is you now being unapologetically woke. We understand at this time that it is important to incorporate positive thinking into your everyday life. Focus on the people that you say that you love and care about. This is not 5,000 people, this is not 50 likes, 100 friends, 2,000 followers, this is going to be a very, very small group. This is going to be three to five people in your inner circle and three to five people in your outer circle. When we are well we realize that we don't have time for a lot of people. We can absolutely leave everyone with a positive thought and a positive verbal compliment that is thoughtful, heartfelt, and encouraging. But at this time, our focus is on centering ourselves and being a positive force for family and for our loved ones.

If you are in a cause not just a job then you're also focused on having confidence and standards to promote your cause. We are always selling confidence.

Anxiety: Curing the New Normal

Your standard is how you work, you have your standards, and no one can change them. Define them and you cannot compare yourself with others. You must know your best, do your best, and be your best; it is personal and it is private.

I once had a patient who was at the top of his selling game. He sold a very luxurious product. He was very proud of it and he won top salesperson year after year. After he had a child he came to see me to look at his fears and anxiety around his consciousness as a parent. After we worked out of his anxiety he realized that he no longer cared to be the top salesman. Although he loved his profession he just wanted to do the best and focus more on the enjoyment of the people around him. Much to his surprise in the end he was still the salesman of the year. He kept his standards but found the joy and passion while learning to set boundaries and go home and see the people that he loved.

This system has required a lot of you. It required that you look deeply and dig out the pains that have kept you small and that have kept you from living your best life. It might seem as though I'm asking for perfection but it is time. In America our children are being emotionally ignored. The abuse is so normalized. It is time that we take a look at ourselves and the subtleties of creating a generation of anxious and depressed human beings. We are not even close to getting a passing grade. I am asking that you strive for an "A." What I'm asking you to do in the end is to follow nature which has always been here for us and it always will. Follow your 5-point self-care each and

The Treatment

every day, talk about it with others and teach it to those you care about. It will keep you centered.

If you have taken your time in reading this book and you are entering the "brick-drying year" give yourself time to let your feelings catch up to your thoughts. This is sometimes a concern when you have been in the dark for so long and the lights come on, you don't know what you are looking at, but you will. Give your heart and soul time to adjust. During your year in the light, re-read this book and reflect on your notes. How have you changed? What is different about your feelings? Are you happy?

I wish you inner peace and the strength to give it to others.

I believe in you and the world needs you.

About the Author

Gina Herd is an artist, athlete, and a licensed therapist who has spent the last 20 years reflecting how and why we have anxiety and depression. She has a background in the arts (music and performance). Her system is unique in that it combines many techniques and methods to get rid of anxiety and stabilize depression. Her method gets to the root of anxiety in a way that is easy to understand on your journey to find relief and inner peace.

Gina believes that having clear measurable goals are important for staying focused and seeing progress.

https://ginaherdlcsw.com

Made in the USA
Middletown, DE
03 August 2023